WHERE IS ADAM?

UNDERSTANDING
A FATHER'S ROLE

WHERE IS ADAM?

UNDERSTANDING
A FATHER'S ROLE

by

Jeff Wheeler

Front Cover Design and Illustration by Doug Knutson

ISBN: 061595863X

Mr. Wheeler is available for speaking, and teaching engagements, where concepts from "Where is Adam's" accompanying Workbook can be shared. Please visit our web site @ Whereisadam.org for more information.

Dedication

I would like to dedicate this book to all the parents who are raising their children in such a way that they will be equipped and prepared for an exciting future that awaits them, a future where they push limits and boundaries to new heights. I also want to acknowledge all those who have stepped up to the plate and are raising nieces and nephews, grandchildren and great grandchildren, foster children and adopted children, and to those who have taken in young people and treated them as their own (Uncle and Aunt Palmer, I thank you from the bottom of my heart). All of you are the true heroes of life. To those who mentor and tutor, coach, guide and encourage young people, thank you, and may God bless you one hundred fold for your efforts.

To my boo (wife) thank you for your undying support and encouragement as I took time while at home, and on vacation to put my emotions to print, you never once complained. Thanks to my friends and family for listening and encouraging me on this project. You were my village.

Thanks, to Pastor Jennings, Minister Benman, Sidney Oliver, Attorney Gerald Snodgrass, Attorney Anthony Maxwell, Mr. Powell, Mark Miller, Mark Williams, Chris, Jorgina, Ladilia Postel for your support and positive words of affirmation. Thanks Jo Jo for lighting a fire under me and for crying and laughing with me as we read this book together. Oh! And thanks for being the first to "get it" by becoming a Big Sister! You are awesome.

To my friend and mentor, Master Mike Wilson, for taking this journey with me and giving me much inspiration and feedback and always staying positive. To Nik Skinner for keeping me accountable. Lastly to my dear children, Quion, Osai, Quaina, and Quiara, thank you for the awesome Father's Day gift, I will never forget it as long as God gives me breath. If I missed anyone, charge it to my head and not my heart.

TABLE OF CONTENTS

Reflections

The man that I turned out to be has a direct correlation and connection to the relationship that I had with my father. What he said, or did not say, what he did, or did not do has affected me to this day.—Jeffrey Wheeler

When one man stands, he strengthens the spines of others.—Author unknown.

Our children don't need us to be their friends; they need us to be their parents! Anthony Maxwell Sr, Prosecuting Attorney.

The best way to raise a man is to be taught by one.—Pastor Marvin A. Jennings Sr., Senior Pastor, Grace Emmanuel Baptist Church.

Some inappropriate behavior is considered to be cute and even amusing by their parents when their children are very young. However, that same behavior becomes ugly as the child ages and socially unacceptable as the child grows into adulthood. Unfortunately for the boys and girls who commit these actions, they weren't taught the error of their ways. As a result, they did not learn or understand the significance of their offense. IT BOILS DOWN TO PARENTING!—Sidney Oliver, School District Behavioral Specialist, Mentor, Gospel Musician.

There was a time when a group of boys were afraid to enter in to the presence of a group of men. The opposite is now true today. —Author unknown.

Most people in our society tend to act based on the influences of what they have seen or heard. Few people really know what it takes to actually be themselves. To be or not to be, that is the question.—Brian Willingham, Police Officer, Author, Poet and Community Activist.

Preface

I must say that I have been inspired to write this book for many years. It is a literary journey that was birthed from life's experiences and the twenty-three years that I spent as a police officer for the City of Flint Police Department. While employed in Flint, Michigan, I was assigned to several bureaus within the Department, but none has left more of an effect on me than the seventeen years that I was assigned to the Liaison, or what's now called the School Resource Program. This historical program between the City of Flint and the Flint Community School District represents a relationship that spans over fifty years. It is a program that has been so successful that it has been sought after and duplicated by many departments and school districts across our great country. It is a comprehensive program where police officers work with school administrators and their teaching staff, parents and their children/students, judges, attorneys, and various other agencies—just about anyone that's connected to juveniles.

As a police officer, I have mentored and counseled literally thousands of children and teenagers (and parents as well). My attempt was to divert these kids from the perils that were so eagerly awaiting them on the harsh streets of not only Flint, but life as well. I wanted to show them options that would steer them from a life that would lead them to juvenile detention and, ultimately, the already overcrowded prison system. I believe that I have been more successful than not in this endeavor, all the while realizing the old adage: "You can lead a horse to water, but you can't make him drink." I can say with conviction that no one can accuse me of not leading him or her to the water.

During my career of almost a quarter century, I have arrested approximately 1500 young people. If that does not disturb you, it should because it disturbed me. That's one thousand and five hundred school-age children I've arrested or taken into custody, and some were as young as six years-old! These arrests have varied from running away from home, to delinquency, truancy, various misdemeanor offenses as well as serious felony crimes, such as assault with intent to murder, carjacking and various gun charges and everything in between. As one could imagine, I grew weary of this part of my job early in my career and began to seek out an alternative method to effect change. I knew that there had to be something else, so I began to focus more on prevention, intervention, and mentoring. I learned very quickly that you can't always change a young person's behavior by arresting him/her and locking him/her down. The courts were already bursting at the seams with juvenile cases. It seemed that the only thing that was working well was the revolving door. It was as if the kids walked in the front door and out the back. What I saw and experienced was juvenile after juvenile given a proverbial slap on the wrist and returned to the streets. Many times, they would commit worse crimes or fall victim to their own folly which often ended in their untimely and tragic deaths. It has been said that when you lose an adult, you lose the story from a great book. But, when you lose a child, you lose the library.

But in the courts' defense, what are they supposed to do? Lock up every kid that makes a mistake or commits a crime? Do you think that's reasonable? Do you think that is the answer or solution, to lock up all of our kids? And after all, how much of what they do is really their fault? Now, please don't misunderstand me. I most certainly believe in personal responsibility, and I advocate that the proper consequences and disciplines are meted out for the offense. Otherwise, how else will a person learn that what s/he has done is unacceptable? Most of the young people that I've come into contact with who found themselves in trouble really didn't have a clue. They simply didn't know any better or didn't have the strength to do better. I soon discovered that these troubled kids suffered from a key missing ingredient. That missing link, at least in my mind, was and is a father.

I've learned that if you want to change a person's behavior, you must change that person's way of thinking because most people are held captive, not so much by their environment, but by their mind set. Stinking thinking has killed more dreams and opportunities than ghettos ever have. I also read somewhere: Be careful what you hear and see because it will affect your thoughts. Your thoughts will affect your actions. Your actions will affect your habits, and your habits will ultimately determine your destiny. I don't think that most kids understand this principle because a great number of them have seen and heard a lot, much of which they should never have been exposed to. It's no wonder they make the choices that they do.

The opportunity for change comes when you show these misguided children a different way, when you say what you mean as well as show them that you care. They need someone who will listen as well as they talk. And for goodness sake, model good behavior so that there is no confusion as to what they are being told. The day of "do as I say and not as I do" is long gone, don't you agree? I read somewhere that people don't care how much you know, until they know how much you care.

If you haven't figured it out yet, this is not a book of answers. This book is intended to raise questions such as, "What can I do to make a difference?" "What could I have done differently?" "What can I say to young people that will possibly help them along their way and maybe even prevent them from making the same mistakes that I have made?" (And we've all made them; right?) It is also my hope that the questions raised will motivate and create a sense of personal involvement that will lead to solutions, solutions that can be deposited into the life of a child who is in dire need of the knowledge and attention that only you can give. This is a book of reflections and foresight, a book that takes a look at despair, but offers hope as well. This is a book that will, hopefully, bring about a desire to do something about this tremendous challenge and bring about a much needed change in the life of a child.

I'm sure that you may be wondering; "What can I do? I'm not a part of an institution or agency that deals with kids." Well, you may not be connected to anything or anybody that has anything to do with kids, but you can still help. I'm here to tell you that you can still be a great influence. There were those that influenced me, as I am sure there were others that influenced you in some positive way.

CHAPTER ONE

I WANT MY MOMMA

I'm reminded of a sad scene. Some years ago there was a senseless murder committed by two or three teenagers. I don't recall all the details but what sticks out in my memory is watching the news of the courtroom scene as these young people were being sentenced. It's actually quite sad. To the best of my recollection, the story unfolds with an innocent man being gunned down and robbed in his front yard. The suspects were eventually arrested for this heartless crime charged as adults and found guilty. If I recall correctly the suspects were in their mid- to late-teens. Only one of the young people actually pulled the trigger that killed this man, but the others were charged as accomplices. In the end they all received the same sentence, 25 to life! There were four lives destroyed the day of the crime: The innocent victim and the three young men. Understandably, many people didn't have much sympathy for the three young suspects involved in this heinous crime. But their lives had value as well. Unfortunately, they did not recognize it.

The exact details of the crime are fuzzy, but what I do remember very clearly, was, as I followed this case, that these young men appeared to have a rather nonchalant and even cocky attitude about what they had been accused of. But when they were found guilty and the reality of going to prison began to sink in, their menacing demeanor changed. You could see fear, confusion, and panic all over their faces. When the verdict was finally passed down, the courtroom violently erupted as friends and family members tried to reach out and console these now fear-stricken boys who were literally being carried off by the court officers. What stood out like a light in a dark room was that one of the young boys began to yell: "I want my Momma! I should have listened Momma! I should have listened to you!"

I wonder if this young man were saying he wanted his mother when he made the decision to get into the car that day. I wonder if he were saying, "I want my Momma," as he and his friends ran across that innocent man as he was cutting his grass. I wonder if he wanted his mother when the shot was fired that took the life of a man that had as much of a right to life as they did. Unfortunately, for Momma she would not be able to help him on the day he needed it most.

When the verdict was passed down on these boys and the commotion began to escalate in the courtroom, extra sheriff deputies were called in for support. And speaking of support,. for these young men, it appeared that support was something that was severely lacking in their lives. After watching that horrible scene unfold, it was obvious that as much as their mothers desperately wanted to help their children, all they could do was stand by as they were carried off to prison. I wonder where the fathers of these young men were. It's apparent that they were absent in the court room. Were they absent from their lives? Were they in prison themselves? Were they dead? I don't know the details, but I can only assume the worst. There is one thing that we can't leave to assumption, and that is that things will get better or change without the intervention of fathers and strong responsible men who will step up to the plate and do their jobs as leaders in their homes and communities. I hope and pray that this book will be a tool that will help bring about that change.

CHAPTER TWO

WHO AM I?
(I AM NOT WHO THEY SAY I AM)

As we all know, our experiences not only vary from culture to culture but also from person to person. It is from those experiences that we are shaped, molded, and, as some would say, "wired." In the study of human behavior, we are told that the influences we are exposed to in our early developmental years (from birth to about six years of age) will shape us foundationally for the rest of our lives. There are others that suggest that we will become products of our environment, and most of us will not move past those influences. Then, there are others that disagree with this theory. For example, if Papa were a rolling stone, it's a great possibility (according to the first theory) that I will repeat that same behavior. Or will I? That same school of thought says that if Momma were a substance abuser or alcoholic, I most certainly will be doomed to the same fate. There are some who suggest that substance abuse can be a part of your genetic makeup, while others say that it is disease. I once heard a radio talk show host say, "Every malfunction of society has been deemed a disease these days. And if alcoholism is a disease, it's the only disease that you can buy at a pharmacy and is regulated by the federal government." That was his opinion; what's yours? Are these things as simple as Choice? Why some people are able to make the right choice and others do not seems to be a mystery.

It is not my intent to dispute either of these thoughts or theories, I only want to present a different view realizing that everyone is unique; as different as fingerprints or snowflakes. We may look the same, but our personal experiences have shaped us to be one of a kind. We are the same in many ways, yet we are indeed very different.

For example, both my mother and grandmother were alcoholics and died from alcohol-related ailments, such as cirrhosis of the liver chronic heart disease. There are some who would say that I have the genetics for this drinking demon like I have the genetics for the diabetes that runs in my family. As for the diabetes, I'm still working on that one, but I think I have the drinking thing licked. Now, I'm not knocking anyone who decides to indulge in adult beverages, I have simply chosen not to make it a part of my life.

CHAPTER THREE

CIGARETTE, ANYONE?

I remember the first and last time that I tried to smoke a cigarette (or anything else for that matter). I was about ten years-old at the time and was walking with a friend who offered me a puff from his mother's Benson and Hedges stash. As I succumbed to his peer pressure, I was a little apprehensive about it but thought that I was far enough away from home that I would not get caught by my mother. Unfortunately, for me and my friend, my next door neighbor drove by and saw me coughing and gagging. He stopped his car and gave me a tongue lashing that I will never forget. He put me in his car and took me home. I begged him not to tell my mother to which he agreed if I promised to never do it again.

I have since forgotten his name, but I didn't forget the lesson nor did I forget what he told me about peer pressure. He said, "You be the peer that creates the pressure, be a leader not a follower." I kept my promise on both ends of the deal. I have never attempted to smoke again, and I have had the fortune to be placed in many leadership positions. You see, it's not that my mom never told me in her own way that I should think for myself and make good choices. But when this man said it, it seemed to have much more substance to it. I don't know why, but it just did.

CHAPTER FOUR THE

MAN NEXT DOOR
(The Village)

There was a guy who lived next door to me when I was a kid growing up in Flint. This was during a time when the economy was good and jobs were plentiful. Most of Flint's neighborhoods were thriving, and people were doing pretty well. Also, it was a time when neighbors were instrumental in keeping each other's kids in line and on the straight and narrow. I remember this neighbor, after seeing and hearing the commotion that often went on in our house when my mother would have a little too much to drink, would take the time to encourage me. It was this neighbor who would say things like, "Make sure you watch out for your mother and take care of her." He would also say things like, "Stay strong and stay focused." What amazed me the most was after observing the chaos that was going on in our house; he never said anything negative about my mother. I appreciated that.

One day he told me that life was mostly about choices, he told me that I could choose not to do what my mother was doing. Even though he didn't mention drinking, I knew exactly what he was talking about. Well, that choice thing stuck with me. What he said impacted me in a major way. As for the drinking that ran rampant in my family, was it personal determination? or divine intervention? Was it the fact that I saw what drinking was doing to my mother and grandmother that helped me make the right choice? Or was it the guy next door? These and other thoughts will be visited in this book. I would just like to say that I'm glad that I had someone who at least thought enough of me to give me something to think about. Yes, I think the man next door helped me make the right choice, but the choice was mine to make, and mine alone.

And like that nameless man who helped me, you and I can also single handedly change the direction of a young person's life no matter what they are exposed to or where they come from. Will this happen without challenge? It's doubtful. Will it occur without personal investment? Definitely not. Will you be successful 100 percent of the time? I don't think so. Will you make a difference? Well, I guess that's up to you!

I do believe, however, that a person can be shaped and heavily influenced by the various exposures in his/her early years. And those negative experiences and the absence of positive role models (male or female) can be a major contributor as to why so many children grow up to repeat negative behavior. But I also believe that life is about choices, and for some those choices can be quite difficult. I have come to the conclusion that difficult can be…well, difficult, but at no time is difficult impossible.

We teach our four- and seven year-old students at Double Dragon (the martial arts school I own) that, "Hard is not impossible". A simple concept I know, but, when these students are faced with life challenges, whether it be their ABCs or the pressure to skip school or dabble with drugs or alcohol, they must know and implement this concept. They will be equipped with a mental advantage that will surely help them if they choose to use it. It is my hope that they go on to do great things. But they must be equipped.

As for choices, you can't choose the family that you are born into, no more that you can determine the color of your eyes, hair, skin or your financial condition. These are things that are not in our control. Some say that you have to accept the cards you have been dealt. However simplistic this theory may be, it does hold some truth. But I say if life has given you lemons, make lemonade.

I was speaking with a fifteen-year-old girl not long ago who was a runaway and had been so off and on for about three to four years. She shared her life story with me. Her dad had fathered many children throughout the city and had abandoned her and her other siblings, ultimately splitting the family. This young girl told me how her mother had given her up for adoption before she was old enough to get to know her. Her adoptive mother had given up on her because of her admitted self-destructive behavior. This fifteen year old young lady shared that she had sold her body and stripped in clubs just to survive. As I was talking with this awesome young woman, I shared with her about my relationship with my own teenage daughter. I told her that as a father, my responsibility is to provide for my daughter, to be an example for her, and to protect and love her.

As I was sharing with this young lady, this street-hardened young woman began to cry. Chronologically she was 15, but experientially she was at least twice that. I told her that she had been cheated. Even though she had been adopted by someone who selflessly allowed her into her home and life, she was cheated from the love of her own mother and father. When I said this, she cried even harder. I shared with her that despite this deficit in her life, she could make it and go on to do great things. She told me she had never been told such words. I shared with her that I counted it my responsibility to let her know these things. What she was used to hearing was, "You're going to be just like your father!" What a thing to say to a child! Unfortunately, I hear parents say this to their children often. I have to remind myself that broken people break others! I wonder if her father had been there for her would she be in this position. Would life be different forher? Would she be different? Would she be stripping and prostituting? Despite all of this, I found her to be compassionate, loyal, nurturing, honest, very intelligent, and full of hope. Misguided, but hopeful nonetheless.

Some would say that she was doomed from the start, that she was "dealt a bad hand" in life, that there is no way that she can overcome such odds. But I say where there is a will, there is a way. I have found that in this life, along with the challenges that it can bring, we need more than just a PMA (positive mental attitude) to help us through, more than Prozac or Celeza, and more than Jim Beam or Budweiser. As a Christian, I live my life by a scripture in Philippians 4:13 which states: "I can do all things through Christ who strengthens me."

Thank God for strong mothers and grandmothers, they have held the family unit together for generations. While serving as mother and father, the bread winners and the homemakers, they have had to do it all, and to their credit, they have done a tremendous job. But the job was not designed to be theirs to bear alone. It is supposed to be a shared responsibility. She was supposed to be the "help mate," the finisher or completer. She was supposed to have help.

I have said it many times before, and I'll say it again: "A woman can teach her son to be compassionate. She can teach him to be responsible. She can even teach him to be tough, but she can never teach him to be a man." It takes a man to do that! You cannot give to someone something you do not possess. As a man, I have encountered hundreds, if not thousands, of adult males who have never grown into manhood. They walk and act as children in adult bodies. In each of those cases, I have found that there was a missing component—a strong, responsible, and committed father. They did not have a father to teach them the fundamentals of life. They did not have a father to teach them to carry themselves, how to speak, how to act, how to treat women, and even how to treat other men.

It is my personal belief that who I turned out to be as an adult has many contributing factors. But foundationally, who I am, is directly related to what my father did or did not do, what he said or did not say in my life. To this day I wish that things would have been different between my father and me. I've shared that thought with others who have agreed, and with some who have disagreed, and that's ok. Interestingly enough, through all the conversations and through all the great debates, most, if not all, of us, seemed to come to the same common conclusion: We're definitely better off with a father, than without one.

Whether you agree with my observations and experiences is not really the purpose for this book. We all come from different family backgrounds and experiences and bring different viewpoints that are important and worth listening to. I only want to present the questions, understanding that people will have their own answers. The question will be presented nonetheless, a question that has no simple or easy answers, and that question is, "WHERE IS ADAM?"

CHAPTER FIVE YOU

AIN'T MY DADDY

(If I had a dollar for every time I heard this one!)

It was a warm autumn day at Central High School where I was assigned as a police liaison. We were just about two weeks into the new school year, and, at least for awhile, everyone was still excited about being back in school (sigh...remember those days?). Students were happy to see old friends that they had lost contact with over the summer break and had not yet had time enough to remember or create new grudges and feuds that often followed the start of every school year. Quite naturally everyone was checking out each other's new gear (that's "clothing" for you old timers). The guys were checking out the girls, and the girls were checking out the guys. It was a good day. No one appeared to be thinking about bashing each other's head in, which made for a even better day for me. I was even greeted with hugs, high fives and handshakes. Life was good!

The teachers and administrators were yet to be stressed out by ill-behaved students and their angry parents who seemed to blame them for their children's poor grades and behavior. There was talk of the upcoming football game against some third-rate team that the students were sure they were going to defeat, and, of course, let us not forget the home coming dance! There was talk about who was going with whom and what was going to be the hottest outfit that year. Talk of who was going to be voted homecoming king and queen filled the air. Everyone seemed to be happy, or so it seemed.

It was the second lunch period and, as was my lunch routine, I was perched in the cafeteria with the kids as they ate, talked, and laughed. I made sure that the students saw me just in case there were any problems brewing. Most, if not all, of the kids knew better than to argue or fight when I was around, and, for the most part, they behaved themselves. But after all, this was a new school year, and there was bound to be a new student or two that had not yet been briefed on how things were run when I was around.

I didn't feel any tension in the air until a young man (we'll call him Joe), whom I didn't recognize, walked into the cafeteria. As Joe looked around for, perhaps, a familiar face, it was also obvious that he was new to the school and may have felt out of place. For one, he was about fifteen minutes late, and, two, he appeared to be a little older than the students that were in the lunch room.

I watched as Joe scanned the room until he apparently saw someone he knew. He then walked over to a group of boys I recognized as being returning students from the previous school year. Whether or not they were friend or foe was soon to be discovered. I recognized one of the boys in the group from an arrest I made towards the end of the previous school year for fighting in the parking lot. I happened to run into that young fella during the summer, and he told me how stupid he was for fighting, and apologized for his actions. When Joe got near the other boys, they all stood up, which was not a good sign.

All the students and staff instinctively knew that when the sound of multiple chairs scraped across the floor, you better believe there was about to be trouble. Of course, this commotion immediately upset the balance that had been set in the room. Warm thoughts of football and homecoming had quickly been replaced with, "It was time to get down and dirty." Everyone knew one or two things were about to happen, a fight or someone was going to get arrested!

Students knew that if I caught them fighting, especially

in the cafeteria or where large groups of people were, they were going to get arrested and at least 10 days suspension from school or worse. When the students stood up, they looked in my direction, as if to say, "Officer Wheeler, you need to get over here because something bad is about to happen!" They had been trained well.

Joe began to call the young man out and punk (challenge) him in front of the other boys that he was sitting with at the table. As is the nature of my job, the mood had shifted from calm to chaotic in the blink of an eye, from warm and fuzzy to a fighting frenzy. By now, half of the cafeteria had stood up in anticipation of the year's first fight.

The young man had obviously allowed Joe to affect his short-term memory (remember the apology?) and get the better of his sense of judgment. After being called a few more names by Joe, he stepped out from the safety of his entourage. By that time, I was heading across the room, which was met with, "Here comes Officer Wheeler! Ya'll better sit down!"

As I got closer, the young man that was called out shouted in my direction, "Officer Wheeler you better get him!" The newcomer not knowing my reputation with the students, didn't seem the slightest impressed. He continued calling the boy out. Just when he was about to punch the young man, I grabbed him around his waist, pinned his arms against his sides, and walked him out of the cafeteria. This was met by applause by those who were glad the peaceful moment wasn't totally ruined and boos from those who wanted to see a good fight.

As I was walking Joe out, he continued struggling and cursing, demanding that I let him go. Once we were outside the cafeteria doors away from the crowd, I let him go and said, "Son, it isn't that serious; calm down!" When I called him "son," you would have thought I talked about his dear sweet grandmother that was on her death bed somewhere. Joe balled up his fist, puffed up his chest, and glared at me with all the hate and hurt he could muster. Then, he took a step toward me and punched at me. I parried his punch and put him in a come-along hold and walked him on his tippy toes toward my office where I could decide what I was going to do with this angry, hurt, and out of control young man. As we were walking up the steps to my office, Joe kept repeating over and over, "You ain't my daddy! Let me go! You ain't my daddy. Let me go!"

He was so loud that teachers were coming out of their class rooms to see what the commotion was all about. Once they saw that it was me, they knew things were under control and went back into their rooms. Once in my office, I placed Joe in a chair and told him to calm down. As he was sitting there rubbing his arm, he continued to huff and puff like he had just run the one hundred yard dash. He still had his fist clenched and his nostrils flaring. I suggested that he calm himself and take as much time as he thought he needed. While he was trying to gather himself, I sat quietly at my desk across from him with my hands folded, waiting for this temper tantrum to pass.

I must say that normally I would have requested that the principal suspend him, at which time he would have been marched out to my awaiting police cruiser and taken to jail. Yet, somehow today was different. I don't know if I were feeling especially generous or if I were getting soft. What I sensed from Joe was more hurt than anything else, and going to jail was not what he needed at this point. So I waited for what seemed like an hour for him to settle down. When he finally got himself together, I asked him what was wrong. He told me that this was his first day at Central, and he didn't want to be there. He told me that he was 18 years old and just got out of lockup and the judge ordered that he had to go back to school or he was going to send him off to boot camp.

Well, apparently my senses were right; it appeared that Joe was just looking for a reason to go back before the judge. He then began to tell me how the boy he was trying to fight in the cafeteria lives in his neighborhood, and, before he was locked up, they had fought over some rumors that were going around in the neighborhood.

Joe continued to attempt to convince me how tough he was by stating that he wasn't scared of no one, and as soon as he got a chance he was going to get the other boy and anyone else that got in his way. While Joe was talking, I interrupted him and stated, "Where's your father?" When I said that, he instantly became angry again. I asked him again, and once again he said, "I told you. I ain't got no daddy." This time I didn't let him off the hook. I told him that he may not like his father and he may even hate his father or it could be that he didn't know who his father was, but he surely had one. That statement seemed to strike a chord with Joe. It make him think and calmed him down. I guess he had no choice but to reason through my statements, which were simply a matter of fact. Joe told me his daddy was in jail and he didn't want to talk about it. Then, I asked another question, a question I have asked countless young men over the years, and that question was: "Are you trying to go to prison like your father?" Then, he glared at me with contempt, and, with all the sarcasm he could muster, he said, "Naw! I don't want to go to prison like my father." It was obvious that a connection was made with him. I then told Joe, "It's not what a person says that matters most in life; it's what he does! Even though you say you're not headed to prison, your actions demonstrate that you are." Once again Joe paused, as if to digest this strange dialogue that he was experiencing. I don't think he was expecting the responses he received from me. It was then that he seemed to soften up a little. I think I was getting though to him.

Then, I told Joe, "You're heading somewhere even if it's nowhere, and you're going to be someone, even if it's no one." At that point he broke down and started to cry. It was apparent that crying was something that he was not used to doing. He, then, told me that his mother has always told him that he was going to be just like his "no-good" daddy. I asked him where his mother was, and he shared with me that she was on the streets. The courts made him live with his aunt until he finished school. He said that his aunt was nice enough but she didn't know how to deal with him so he did pretty much as he pleased. I asked if his uncle were around, but he shared that he didn't see his uncle much because his aunt and uncle were divorced.

The conversation had now taken a much calmer turn. I told Joe that I was a father of three children. I asked him if he ever thought if he would be a father one day. When I asked that question, he seemed to light up with curious excitement. He told me that he would like to have a son some day. I asked him, "Who is going to teach your son how to be a man? Joe seemed confused with my question, so I asked it again. This time, with defiance and a bit of uncertainty in his voice, he said, "I am." I asked him, how, "How are you going to teach him how to be a man if he you don't know yourself?" Joe paused for a moment, crossed his arms as if he were thinking of a good answer to give, an answer he and I both knew he didn't have. I asked him again. Joe looked quietly out the window and with tears streaming down his face, his answer finally came. It was simply, "I don't know."

CHAPTER SIX

LET ME SHOW YOU HOW

(You can lead a horse to water, but you can't make him drink)

Even though this book was not supposed to be all about Joe, I thought you might like to hear the rest of the story and how it ends. So where did we leave off? Oh yea, I gave Joe all the time he needed to release whatever was inside him. When it was clear that he had regained his composure, Joe seemed to have turned into an entirely different person. It was eerie to see this transformation, from absolute rage, to tears, to a passive lamb all in a matter of an hour. It was as if he experienced a release of some sort, a release that was a long time coming. Looking back, I'm glad that it happened with me.

Joe told me that because he was always bigger than most people his age, he had turned into somewhat of a bully, and he was ok with that. Picking on people was easy to do, that was the way he expressed himself. It worked on the streets, and being in the streets was all he really knew, that and detention facilities.

I shared with Joe that, "You don't know what you don't know. And how can a person know something different unless someone shows them?" The room grew quiet for a moment, and it appeared that Joe was perplexed about something. Once again my senses were right, and he asked me why I didn't pepper spray him and take him to jail when he was trying to jump on the other student in the cafeteria. I told him I chose not to because I felt there was something more important that needed to be done, and jail wasn't it. He shook his head as if to say, "That's not what I would've done." He then told me that he didn't understand, especially after he took a swing at me, stating that he deserved to go to jail; as a matter of fact, that's why he did it. Well, Joe had a point, I've arrested people for less, but it just didn't feel right.

At the end of the school day I decided to take Joe home. As I was walking him to my police cruiser, apparently word had spread around the school about the new kid getting handled by Officer Wheeler. I guess they thought that he was going to be the first arrest of the new school year. By rights he should have. The students seemed to be a bit confused. Instead Joe being hand cuffed and placed in the rear of my cruiser, he was walking on his own and taking a seat in the front. I must be slipping!

Over the coming weeks, I noticed Joe attending school on a regular basis. It appeared that he was trying to fit in, and, as far as I could see, he was doing a pretty good job at it. I can say that I had not heard of him getting into anymore trouble, but I also noticed that he was wearing pretty much the same clothes every day. After about a month or so, it was apparent that he was not attending class regularly, so I called his aunt and asked her if she knew if he were going to school. She informed me that as far as she knew he was heading out to school each day. Then, I shared with her that, since I had not seen him in several days, I took the liberty to check with some of his teachers and found that his attendance had taken a turn for the worse.

She seemed worried, so I told her that I would check into it. The next day, I went to work early and parked down the street from Joe's house in my other unmarked car. It was about six-thirty in the morning on an early fall day. As I was sitting there, just as I suspected, Joe came out of the house and headed toward the bus stop as if he were going to school. When he knew his aunt wasn't looking, he went the other way. I followed Joe at a distance and noticed that he met up with some other boys on the corner; they all then headed to a vacant home a few blocks from his house. When I figured they were settled in, I entered the house and found Joe smoking cigarettes as three other young men were smoking and playing dice. When they saw me, I recognized two of the boys to be drop outs from another Flint high school. They must have remembered the unpleasant encounter we had experienced at a football game in the fall. Because without being commanded, they both put their hands against the closest wall while the third boy ran out the room falling over trash as he jumped out a broken window.

After giving the two boys the riot act, I kicked them out of the vacant house and sent them on their way. While this was going on, Joe was standing with his mouth wide open as if to say, "How did you find me?" Then, I told him to get in my car, and we headed off to school. While we were enroute, he said, "I know what you're thinking, 'what was I doing in a vacant house and why wasn't I in school.' " At that point Joe proved to be a psychic; maybe he was smarter than I thought he was. So instead of saying something that I would regret, I took the fifth and remained silent as we headed back to Central High School. It was a long ride.

Once we arrived, I took him back to my office where he sat in the same chair where we had our first encounter. After a few minutes of uncomfortable silence, I asked Joe why he wasn't in school when he knew full well that the judge told him that he must stay in school or he was going to get sent off to boot camp. Then, Joe told me he wasn't trying to get into trouble, but he was embarrassed because he had to wear the same clothes almost every day.

Well, I understood that kids could be cruel about such things, so I told him that I was going to work on his clothing problem. I told to see me at the end of each class and, again, at the end of the school day. When he left the office, I called my wife and shared the situation with her. She told me to do what I needed to help Joe. So, at the end of the school day, I canceled my plans, and Joe and I took a ride to a local department store.

I don't think Joe had been school shopping in quite some time. First of all, he had no idea what size he wore, and, secondly, he was like a kid in a toy store. This 18 year-old was literally running from aisle to aisle grabbing everything he could stuff in the basket, and it didn't matter if it fit or not. Luckily, I had a friend that was a manager at the store, and he gave me a great discount. I didn't have the heart to tell Joe to put anything back. I bought shirts. I bought pants. I bought sweaters, a winter coat, shoes, hats, gloves, even underwear and socks, everything that you or I would buy for our children for school, Joe was provided with. Now, that I look back, I'm sure that I made the right decision not arresting him which would have surely sent him off to boot camp. Instead, it cost me $500 to keep him out of jail, ouch! Yeah, I'm sure I made the right choice. I think.

Things were going well for Joe. His aunt was very grateful for the investment I was making in him; she told me that the attention I was giving him seemed to be paying off. All he talked about was Officer Wheeler this and Officer Wheeler that. She jokingly told me that I was kind of getting on her nerves. I hoped she was joking. She shared with me that, even though she was telling him the same things I was, he seemed to listen to me more. I told her that all parents experience that, that was why it took a village to raise a child. She even shared that he wasn't staying out as late anymore.

Joe was also holding up his end of the bargain in school by going to class every day and staying out of trouble, which was a miracle in itself. His grades were actually improving, and he somehow managed to bring his grades up from all Es the first marking period, to four Cs and an E the second marking period. Not bad for a kid who was reading at a 6th grade level! But I had to ask him, of all classes, to get an E in, how did he flunk gym? He told me that he got an E because he hated to run. I told him he should've gotten an A in gym as much as he used to run from the police. I told him to do what the teacher asked him to do and suck it up.

The biggest surprise was that Joe actually made a friend that he wasn't trying to pound into the ground. Things were going pretty well. The holidays had come and gone. We were now heading into spring with the excitement that the new season brought. Joe had also turned 19 at the start of the New Year, and I told him that he needed to think about getting a job. I told him that he would feel good about himself knowing that he could save for his own school clothes for the upcoming school year, and maybe even start putting away some money for a used car. I told him if he saved up enough money for the car I would help him pay for his driver's training. He thought that was a good deal (at least the car part) and agreed. I was fortunate to get Joe a job at a local fast-food restaurant. He was on his way, or so I thought.

As the weather got warmer, I noticed that I would find Joe outside on the front stoop when he should have been in class. He said that he was just getting some sun in between classes. Well, that front stoop experience turned into getting some sun while he was walking down the street skipping class. It goes without saying that his attendance got worse and his grades began to slip. Also, I noticed that his attitude was changing.

About a week after the first front stoop encounter, I saw Joe loitering in the hallway when he should have been in class. I told him to see me in my office. He showed up; he sat in his usual seat as I sat in a chair next to him. I asked Joe what was going on and why the change in attitude. What Joe told me next was a blindsided sucker punch that I didn't see coming. With all the courage he could muster, Joe said, "I'm 19 now. I'm grown; if I don't want to go to class, I'm not going!" I couldn't believe what I was hearing.

Knowing that Joe was no longer a ward of the court, he was right! He didn't have to continue going to school if he didn't want to. After all being 19, he could just leave, and no one could do a thing about it. The old Joe seemed to reappear, but why? What had changed? He politely asked me if I were finished and stood up as if to leave. Without answering his question, the police officer in me took a back seat, and the father in me stepped to the forefront. Then, I told Joe to sit his butt down. I, then, told him that I didn't spend all that money buying him school clothes, getting his hair cut, and buying him lunch on countless days for him to walk the streets. Joe glared at me with a look that took me back to our first encounter on that warm autumn day. This time the look wasn't just angry, it seemed to be mixed with confusion as well; the words that came out of his mouth hit me like a ton of bricks, words that I had heard countless times before, but for some reason this time the words hurt. Joe said, "I told you; you ain't my daddy."

Well, I know what you're thinking—what the heck just happened? All that you did for that kid, the time you spent, the money you spent, the opportunities you gave him, and that was the way he treated you?

Man, it can be people like that that make you not want to help anyone. It's like the folks who stand on the corners with the "will work for food" signs, only to go around the corner and get into a car nicer than the one you drive. Man, I'll never do anything for anyone else again. That JERK!

Stop the presses! Before we write Joe off and send him to the gas chamber, can I add something? I contacted his aunt. She told me that all Joe used to talk about were the things that I was doing for him. She shared with me that his father had been calling lately and was apparently filling his head with garbage. She told me that she got into arguments with the father because he was telling Joe that he could do whatever he wanted since he had turned 19, especially since he was released from the court's custody.

She said that he started slipping back into his old habits by staying out late and hanging around his old friends. When asked why she didn't call *me*, she said that I had already done enough, and, after all, he wasn't my responsibility. Those words were like a slap in the face, slapping me back to reality. Could I have done more? You know the more I think about it; maybe I should have arrested his behind when I had the chance. Maybe that's what he needed to begin with.

I'm reminded of a seed that's planted in bad soil. Is it the seed's fault or the soil if the plant is deformed when it grows? Whose fault is it? If you transplant that damaged plant, put it in good soil, water it, nurture it, and give it plenty of sun, will it later grow and blossom as it was designed? Was anything I did for Joe really wasted? Or was it just delayed? This particular story didn't end the way most of us would have liked, but who is to say that the story is over? Here's a question for you: As for arresting Joe, if it were you, what would you have done?

Unlike many boys, Joe had two men in his life; two Adams, if you will, one behind bars and one with bars on his uniform. I guess it goes to show you that no matter where our fathers are, their voice is still important, and they can still have tremendous influence on us.

CHAPTER SEVEN

REDEMPTION

(Nothing of significance has ever been achieved, except by those who have overcome their circumstances.—Edith Barton)

I got a text from London, England today from my son Osai wishing me a Happy Father's Day. Well, he's not really my son, but he calls me "Dad." It just seems right to call him my son. I'm as proud of him as I am my own son, and I noticed that he lights up whenever I introduce him such.   Truth be told, I do it every chance I get. I think it's important for a young man to be called "son"; don't you? It gives him a sense of pride and connection. you know what I mean? But I'm getting ahead of myself. I guess I need to introduce you to Osai, don't I?

When I thought about what to name this next chapter, the title came pretty easily, especially after going through that emotional roller coaster with Joe. I thought that you would like to read something more on a positive note. Around 1998 or so my twins, Quion and Quiana, were about 9 years old when my son came to me and told me he wanted to start taking karate lessons. Well, that's not a problem within itself, but you have to understand we had just finished our third year of swimming lessons, and we were knee-deep in Cub Scouts, soft ball, and any and everything else they wanted to do.

I don't mean to complain. I know that's my job and those were all fun activities but, folks, I was tired. You see I'm not one of those dads who just drop their kids off only to return later and pick them up after their activities are over. Nooo, not me. When my kids were getting their fifth level certificate for swimming lessons, guess who was standing dripping wet huffing and puffing next to them getting theirs? When my daughter wanted to join Daisy Scouts, I thought I was going to be able to sit back, relax, and read the paper while she and the other cute little Daisy Scouts earned their cute little Daisy Scout patches and sold their cute little Daisy Scout cookies! Well, somehow it didn't work out that way, and I got recruited. Just call me "Daisy Dad."

When my son wanted to join Cub Scouts, I thought I was going be able to sit back with the other dads and talk about— you know, man stuff, and brag on my boy. Well, that didn't work out either (at least for the sitting back part). Somehow I ended up being the third base softball coach, the popcorn coordinator, and whatever else was needed, and, of course, hauling boys to whereever the next mission was. Now, he wanted to do karate!? Please... What next, skydiving? Folks, I was tired! After a long day at work, I had no energy left for nothing else, especially kicking and punching! I just wanted to sit down and relax. Ok, you've discovered my deep dark secret, guilty as charged, I'm a bad parent.

Well, I shared that part of the story not to talk about my great kids or how tired I was because I know that I'm not alone in that boat, but I brought it up to introduce another young person that I met as a result of joining karate with my kids. He was young man who would soon become as much a part of my family as my own children. His name, Osai (pronounced Oh-si-uh).

It was around early summer of 1999 while we were sweating in karate class doing our best rendition of Chuck Norris and Bruce Lee. I noticed a skinny little boy with an older girl, peaking in the front window watching class. That boy turned out to be an 11 year-old kid named Osai. The young lady turned out to be his aunt, Terina. Funny thing, as soon as we would stop our fists of fury and direct our attention toward them, they would evaporate like smoke blowing in the wind and take off. The next day it started all over again, and I noticed that they had returned to our small store front karate studio. Instead of coming in the door, they sheepishly pressed their faces against the window in an attempt to see through the steam that had covered the windows. I guess they didn't understand that the moisture was on the inside, not the outside. At any rate, on one particular day, they somehow mustered enough courage to at least stand in the doorway, but, once again, as soon as we would turn to acknowledge them, they would disappear. After this cat and mouse game went on for about a week or so, they finally made it through the door where they came in and sat and watched the classes. Well, that experience turned into both Osai and his aunt not only joining the karate studio, but our hearts as well.

I soon learned that Osai's father died when he was very young and he was living with his mother, his Aunt Terina, and younger brother about one quarter of a mile from the school. The first thing that I noticed about this young man was that he was much older than his years would indicate, and, even though he was only 11 years-old, he had a wisdom and poise about himself that was much older. Oasi took to karate like a fish takes to water, and I took to him as well. Not only was and is he very talented, he possessed a great work ethic, and is the type of person that listens to every word of advice or counsel you give him. He was hungry for knowledge and guidance. Remember Joe?

As Oasi, along with my children, and I developed in the art of Tang Soo Do, my relationship with him continued to grow as well. When he was in the 8th grade I gave him a very nice bike so that he didn't have to walk to school. I later found out that the bike was stolen because he failed to lock it up (which was something that I constantly told him to do). I learned very quickly that he had a rather bad habit of losing and forgetting things; his mother stopped giving him keys to the house when he was very young. Well, some weeks after getting this special bike, as you can imagine, it was stolen from school because, you guessed it, he didn't lock it up. He later told me that he didn't have the heart to tell me that it was stolen because he didn't want to disappoint me.

Osai eventually made it through the ranks in the karate school we were attending and was promoted to first degree black belt. In the spring of 2004, my children and I decided to leave our original school where we had been training since 1999, and open our own school called Double Dragon Tang Soo Do which I named after my children. That was the good thing; the bad thing was we were leaving Osai behind to train with our old instructor. For me it was like leaving one of my children behind, but he and his aunt were loyal to my old instructor and friend, Master Michael Wilson. It was Master Wilson along with another mentor who convinced me that it was time to move on and start my own school. So with their blessing and encouragement, that's exactly what I did. It's amazing what you can accomplish with faith, vision, and support from your friends.

It wasn't long before our new karate studio was up and running, and new students were filing in the door. Yet, there was something (or someone) missing. The good news was all about to change. One day in the spring of 2004 I was paid a visit from Master Wilson who informed me that he was shutting his programs down at the YWCA where we had trained and moving to Arizona. He told me that he wanted me to take his students and further their karate training; he couldn't think of anyone better for the task. I cannot express to you what an honor that was for me; the person that instructed me, now wanted me to instruct his students! Well, as you would have it, we gained about twenty students in a day, and Oasi and his aunt were part of that package, and, as the song writer wrote, we were "back together again."

Back Together Again

It was soon time for Osai to attend high school. It wasn't long before he earned my trust as an instructor at Double Dragon; as a result, I promoted him to second in charge and began paying him for his efforts. Imagine that! A 14-15 year-old running a karate school teaching not only children, but adults more than twice his age! This demonstrated his maturity and competence. These were attributes he carried well. I had watched him now for several years and saw that he was a natural leader and teacher. Because of his outstanding dedication, his attention to his technique and leadership ability, I not only gave Osai the position of Assistant Instructor, I also gave him a key to the school. Things went from good to great! The school was growing, and so was Osai.

As with all young people, it soon became time for him to get his driver's license. Speaking of a license, let me tell you a short story. I'm reminded of the time when I received a phone call in the middle of the night from a police officer telling me that he had a young man claiming to be my son, in the back seat of his squad car. He went on to share with me that my *son* was involved in an accident and wrecked my Chevy Blazer. As the officer was speaking, it was as if my whole life passed before my eyes; my mouth instantly lost all moisture; my heart started racing. I broke out into a cold sweat, and I couldn't think straight. My mind instantly took me back to when I brought Quion home from the hospital, how precious and small he was. He and his twin sister were six weeks premature and had to spend the first month of their lives in the hospital. I thought about how I promised God that I was going to be the best father in the world. I recalled how I potty trained him, how I taught him how to tie his shoes, to read and write, and ride a bike and how I taught him how to drive in the parking lot of the high school, how I…. Wait a minute! Quion is only twelve years old, and he's in bed. I know that because he was up not long ago using the bathroom. I don't own a Chevy Blazer! Who is this imposter saying he's my... au, ooh!

Apparently, the officer assumed that I had passed out from shock or had dropped the phone because all I heard on the other end was, "Officer Wheeler, are you there? Are you ok?" When I came back to my senses, the officer was able to tell me the rest of the story. He told me that my son Osai (!) ran a red light while taking his date home from the homecoming dance and t-boned another car. He assured me that there were no injuries but the car would have to be towed. Then, I called Osai's mother and explained to her what had happened and that I would go get the kids. This required me to get out of my warm bed and drive to the accident scene on a cold October night. As the officer said

Oasi was in the back seat of the squad car with his head hung low like a defeated fighter with his date sitting next to him in her pretty homecoming dress with mascara running down her face. What a sight! I can see the headlines now: "Homecoming king and queen spend night in jail after crashing their parents'car." The officer was nice enough to extend to me professional courtesy and allowed me to take both kids home. Before I got into the car, the officer called me over and said, "I thought you only had three kids." I smiled at him and said, "This son is from another mother." Then, I left the officer scratching his head in confusion as we drove away.

Even though it was only a few miles to Osai's girlfriend house, it seemed like we were traveling across the country; the silence was deafening. As we were driving, I asked, "Are you guys ok?" The response was faint but convincing, and in unison they both said, "Yes, Sir." I dropped the girlfriend off safe and sound reassuring her grandmother that things were ok. Then, Osai and I made the long quiet trek across town to his house. Not much was said other than, "You need to be more careful and call me if you need me." As he was getting out of the car, I told him that I would see him in class on Monday. As he was walking toward the door, he looked backed as if to say, "I'm sorry" and "thanks." He waved and went into the house.

Relieved that the nights or, should I say morning's, adventures were over, I returned home to my warm bed and gave my worried wife a synopses of the early morning event. After she was satisfied that everyone was ok, I sighed with a sense of relief, turned over, and went back to sleep.

Ample time had passed since the homecoming disaster and Osai had seemed to have regained his confidence and he now wanted a car for himself. So my wife and I found him a hoopty (old car) which would give him his freedom and independence. He loved that old car. I wish we could say the same. The car was in the shop more than it was on the road! I can say that it got incredible gas mileage because it spent more time being pulled to the shop by my truck than it did on its own power.

When Osai was in the 10th grade, I began to challenge

him more on the importance of his grades which at the time were mediocre at best. He was carrying a 2.0-2.5 GPA. We discussed his future and what his career path should be. After our talk, he kicked it in gear, and, from the middle of his tenth grade year until he graduated, he never earned less than a 3.5 GPA. On more than one occasion, he earned all As! He was so proud when he brought me his report cards. During his tenth grade year, with his mother's permission, we introduced Osai to a college program that our own children were enrolled in at the University of Michigan-Flint. This was a program that afforded minority students academic scholarship opportunities if they met and maintained certain academic requirements while in high school. Needless to say, once enrolled, Osai took full advantage of the program, and went on not only to graduate from high school with honors, but quickly began to mentor others that were entering the same scholarship program he had once entered. Osai has always understood the importance of mentoring, helping, and encouraging others to move passed their challenges. We have a motto on the wall of Double Dragon that says, "You can't possess what you are unwilling to pursue." This motto was something that he exemplified.

As you would imagine, Osai's reputation grew quickly on campus. Just as he had gained the respect and trust from me, also, he gained that same level of confidence from those running the college program he was now a part of. As a result, he was given a paid position to mentor incoming students. Even though he had this new position, he never let it interfere with his teaching responsibilities at Double Dragon. Somehow, Osai was able to manage going to class, staying on the Dean's list, working at the college, teaching at the karate school, and functioning as the president of his fraternity. Oh, did I mention that he tutored students of all ages in math as well on Saturday mornings at the karate studio?

In his junior year, Osai transferred to the main campus in Ann Arbor. He impressed his professors so much that he was offered an internship with a company that specialized in water treatment research and systems. As a result, he was given an opportunity to go to several cities in the United States. After we discussed his options, he chose Kansas City, Kansas. In his senior year, he was presented with another opportunity from the same company where we had another conversation, and, as you read at the beginning of this chapter, he texted me from London, England wishing me a Happy Father's Day. Osai will be in the land of the Queen until the end of the summer. When he returns, he will be finishing up his master's degree in civil engineering at the University of Michigan-Ann Arbor where he will graduate in the spring of 2012 with a degree which was paid for by a full academic scholarship.

There are many other stories that I could share with you, but I think you get the picture. There are those who say I should take a bow because of all the great things that Osai has accomplished. Well, I have never been one to read my own press clippings; I'm too busy for that. I think it's vain to do so, but that's just my opinion. The only thing that Osai owes me is to go on and do great things and help someone else along the way.

At Double Dragon, I teach my Black Belt servant leadership that, if you edify others, they will in turn edify you. Besides, I never attended a class with Osai. Most of the subjects he has taken, I can't even spell. I never took a test for him and never stayed up for hours on end studying. It was he who made the decision to go into the engineering field; he accomplished all those things on his own. Or did he? He could have made different choices, but it appears at this point in his life, he has made the correct ones. Were Joe's choices more difficult than Osai's? Were they more difficult than the choices you or I have had to make? Do you remember the intervention and advice that was given to me by an observant neighbor in my Chapter Three when I was growing up? The same question bears repeating; as it relates to Osai, was it personal determination, divine intervention, or was it just the guy next door? What do you think? Given the same opportunity, what would you do? Oh, by the way, Osai has now achieved the rank of third degree black belt and is the current Grand Champion in the Midwest Region as well as a top three finisher at our World Championships for the past six years.

CHAPTER EIGHT

WHAT IN THE WORLD HAPPENED?

I have often said that if you want to flood a room and drown the occupants in it, you don't have to open the roof and let the water pour down over their heads; that would be too obvious. But, if you let the water seep underneath the door, most people wouldn't notice it until things began to float in the room and the water reached a dangerous level. *Denial usually preceeds desperation.* I once read a book entitled *The Bull Whip Days,* a book that compiled the thoughts and writings of slaves from the 1800s during the dark days of slavery in America. In one of the short stories, there was an elder slave that was lamenting over the fact that the children during that time were becoming more and more defiant and disrespectful. Imagine that! Also, I read in scripture that this was nothing new under the sun.

The gradual and systematic break down of "traditional" family values have been slowly eroding in our country for decades. There are some that say that this change began to evolve in our country during the rebellious times that occurred during the sixties, with its radical expressions and social movements. We want to be free! Fight the power, and so on. Whether or not you believe that it started with Baby Boomers or Generation X,Y, or Z, the breakdown of the family structure has been a slow and methodical yet consistent process throughout the years. It has crept up on us at such a slow pace that the word "traditional" needs to be redefined. What does it mean to be "traditional"? Some are even insulted by the implication of the word. What caused the change? When did it begin? Can we blame it on a particular generation or does it go all the way back to Adam? What do you think?

In 1963, Madelyn Murray O'Hare was successful with a petition that took prayer out of the schools in our country. Was *this* part of the break down? Do you find it strange that you cannot read the Bible or pray in school for fear of offending someone, but you can read it all you want in prison? Remember when the person testifying would put his/her hand on the Bible and swear to tell the truth "so help you God"? The courts of our land at one time recognized the Bible as the moral and ethical code of authority. Our Founding Fathers made mention of God frequently when constructing the Constitution and the laws of our great land. But not now, you can't mention God or prayer unless there is a catastrophic event. Remember 9/11? During that dark time in our country, people were praying on the steps of the State Capital.

Remember paddling or swats? I believe the politically correct word these days is "corporal punishment." This form of corrective action has been outlawed in the school system and many think that they even can't spank their own children without being accused of child abuse. Is *this* part of the breakdown?

During my career I have spoken with hundreds of parents who actually believe that they cannot discipline their children. They feel powerless, helpless, and inadequate when it comes to this crucial area of child rearing. I'd be a millionaire if I had a dollar for every mother that has called the police department and said, "I don't know what to do with my kid, he/she is out of control." When I suggest that they should discipline their children, the statement is universally the same: "If I do, my child will call 911 or Child Protective Services on me." Well, let them call! The shocking part is these calls are not for kids that are fifteen or sixteen; they are for children as young as seven years of age. How can this be? Is that part of the breakdown? Not being able to control a seven year old? What happened? What *didn't* happen is probably the better question to ask. As I have received these calls over the years, it has dawned on me that it's not really the kids. It's parenting, or a lack thereof.

I'd like to share an experience that I had with my youngest daughter. While at her school for her parent-teacher conference, the teacher went on and on about how exceptional my daughter was and what an excellent student she was. I was told about her manners and conduct in class, about how she was a leader, and so on and so on. The complements got to the point that they were actually irritating and embarrassing. I actually had to stop the teacher and explain to her, that even though my wife and I thanked her for her accolades and appreciation for our daughter's behavior, we also felt it necessary to remind her that the attributes she witnessed from our daughter had nothing to do with angelic intervention. It was a result of good old-fashion parenting! The simple fact that we happen to parent *our* children in a day and age when many parents want to be their kids' friends is a wonder. When we happen to be out, we see kids telling their parents what to do. Is that part of the breakdown? We haven't done anything special. My wife and I have simply taught our children to respect their teachers and anyone in authority. We've taught them to be polite, and respectful. We've taught them to say "please" and "thank you" and to treat people the way they want to be treated. Why is that so unusual?

In the teacher's defense, I can completely understand how she feels when she encounters children that know that they are just that. Children! They raise their hands when they want to speak and don't get lippy, disrespectful, or curse them, or other students when things don't go their way. Their first recourse is not violence when a social challenge presents itself. Why? They've been taught at home.

Working in the school system for as long as I have has given me first-hand knowledge and experience to what teachers and administrators have to go through on a daily basis. While working in the capacity as a School Liaison Officer, I've had to intervene in literally hundreds of situations involving students who have gotten out of control. These students had not only threatened and assaulted other students; they had done the same to teachers and administrators, and even their own parents. How did this happen? The number of times that I've been called to the office or to the home of a student who had assaulted his/her mother, grandmother, or other caregiver is too numerous to mention. The number of school arrests I've made of school-aged children over my career is in the hundreds. I've arrested parents for assaulting (not disciplining) their children. I've arrested children for assaulting their parents. In my entire career, I cannot recall one occasion that this occurred when there was a responsible father in the home.

I was at work one day in my assigned school dealing with one of the many conflicts that arise with young people throughout the course of the school day. There was a thirteen-year-old girl that was brought into my office by a teacher because she was involved in yet (another) conflict. This little girl was wearing a uniform dress, but, as she sat in the chair, she had her legs spread wide open as if she were wearing pants. The female teacher that she was with had to keep reminding her the proper way to sit with a dress on. This whole concept seemed to be foreign to the young lady. I later learned that the little girl did not live with either of her parents and was in foster care. How was she supposed to know how to sit when she wore a dress? I don't know why she was in foster care; I don't know what happened to her parents. What I do know is that she was missing the most important part of her growing and educational experience—her parents.

Not to say that her foster parents were not teaching her the fundamentals of life and didn't care for her, but they were at best, temporary. That's not how it's supposed to be, but that's the way it is for a large number of children these days. Who will be there for her in the long run? The state? Who will teach her the things she should know about life, that she can do anything if she puts her mind to it? Who will give her away when that special time comes? It's great that our state and federal government have stepped in to be surrogate parents. But, that's not the way it's supposed to be, but for many that's the way that it is.

As mentioned my wife and I are blessed with a pre-teen and two college-age children who have been a joy to our lives. I have enjoyed the countless times that I have braided my daughters' hair and helped them get dressed for the day. I have enjoyed playing dress up, attending tea parties, and getting my finger and toe nails done by them.

It has beeen a pleasure experiencing how they regularly come to me for affirmation and moral support. They have asked: "Daddy, is this pretty?" "Daddy, does this match?" "Daddy, I got an A on a test," and so on. Don't get me wrong. They go to their mother for many things as well, and I know that the relationship of a mother can never be duplicated. Also, I know that, if there ever came a time that a camera were ever placed in front of them, I probably won't be mentioned (the old, "Hi Mom"). I know that it won't matter if I were the one who ran the miles to help my daughter get into shape for her track meet. Probably, it won't be mentioned that I was the one who worked on my son's swing for hours on end as he prepared for his baseball game. But that's my job; isn't it? True fathers don't do those things for air time or to be noticed by others. I'm proud that I was there for my children, that I taught each of them how to ride a bike, how to tie their shoes, how to count and read, and to go poo poo and pee pee in the pot pot. As a father I was there to tuck them in at night and give them a hug as they went off to school the next day. Yes, a father has a special place in the life of his children, a role that cannot be replaced.

Who's going over the homework? Who's taking care of our kids? Who's teaching our sons how to tie a tie, ride a bike, or hit a baseball? Who will teach them that when you shake hands you use a firm grip and look the person in the eye? Who will teach them how to change a flat tire or keep the lines straight when they cut the grass? Who's teaching them these things? Do you think that these things are important? Who's teaching them that it's not proper to wear their pants around their knees and show their underwear? Who's teaching them about sex? The media? The music they listen to and the movies they watch? Fathers. Who will show them how to treat women? Who will teach them that women are not to be disrespected and treated like sex objects or punching bags?

I'm reminded of the countless domestic violence calls that I have been sent to in my law enforcement career. I have seen the breakdown of the most fundamental aspect of the relationship. They simply did not respect each other. The horrible verbal and physical abuse they demonstrate in front of their children is a crime within itself. We need to recognize that there is more than one victim in these very common occurrences. There are other victims left behind long after the offender has been carted off to jail by the police. It is the children. They are as much a victim in this crime as the one who is physically assaulted, but often times there is no help for these kids except in the most extreme cases.

There are studies that indicate that people who are exposed to second-hand smoke are as susceptible to lung cancer and other ills as the primary smoker. I wonder if there is a study that can show a parallel or correlation to what our children are exposed to in their homes and how it affects them as they grow older. Well, I can tell you that it does. The only study I have to validate this is my professional and life experience. And my experience is, unless there is not some sort of counter experience, some sort of intervention, divine or otherwise with a willingness to change, a good number of these young people who have grown up in this environment will repeat the cycle themselves, not knowing how or why it has reappeared in their own lives. I've heard the old adage that the fruit doesn't fall far from the tree. This may have some truth to it, but, as I stated in the earlier chapter, where there is a will there is a way. It does still boil down to choice.

The motivational creed that is on the wall of our karate school in bold letters says: "*You cannot possess what you are unwilling to pursue.*" If a person wants to have success in life, he or she has to pursue success. If people want to acquire certain possessions, they must pursue them. As strange as it may sound, the same holds true for a stable and happy family; it also must be pursued. However, once it has been acquired, it must be respected, polished, and cherished.

CHAPTER NINE

THEY SHOULD KNOW BETTER
(You Don't Know What You Don't Know)

This chapter was inspired by statements that I have heard from frustrated teachers, administrators, officers, and parents throughout my career. I am sharing this thought as a result of an experience that I just had. I happened to be attending a kick-ball game that my youngest daughter was playing in. As we were walking into the school, there was a mother of three that was walking just ahead of us. She had two children around the ages of five or six, and she was also holding a toddler and doing her best to keep them all in line. Of course, I went ahead of her and opened the door. For some reason my act of kindness seemed to surprise her. What was more surprising was that she didn't say, "thank you." It was almost as if she were saying, "I don't need your help," as she continued toward the gym entrance. Once we arrived to the gym doors, there was a young man sitting at a table taking tickets. The mother, busy with her three children, continued in not realizing that she had to stop and pay for entrance into the game. When she walked past, the young man who could not have been older than twelve or thirteen, said, "Aaye, you gotta pay a dollar, lady." The mother looked at him in disgust and appeared to want to say something to him but apparently thought better. With trying to keep track of her three kids, she managed to reach into her purse and pay the cost of admission.

When it was my turn to be greeted by this less than cordial young man, he held out his hand and looked at me as if I should have gotten the message that he had just given the woman that was before me. What I wanted to do to the young man was take off my belt and adjust his attitude (with syllables) but thought that wasn't the best idea. So before paying him the dollar, I decided to give him something much more valuable than the price of admission. What I gave him was priceless. I gave him wisdom. I said, "Young man, the proper thing for you to have said to that woman was 'excuse me, Ma'am; it costs a dollar per person to come into the game." The look he gave me spoke for itself, a look that I am all too familiar with. You do know that you can say a lot without opening you mouth, don't you? Without speaking, he said, "Who do you think you are telling me what to do? You ain't my daddy." The mother with three children looked back at me, this time with a sense of gratitude. I paid the dollar and followed in behind her and took my seat as the young man glared at me with all the contempt he could muster.

Was this young man a bad kid? That remains to be seen, and in his defense I really didn't get a chance to talk to him to find out. But if first impressions mean anything, he did not leave a very good one. Come to think of it, he's probably not the only one guilty of that one, is he?

I have often said that you don't know what you don't know, and to assume that someone knows what you know shows that you don't know very much. Admittedly, this is not a very profound statement, but you must admit it still holds some truth. It has often behooved me how people put their moral standard and stamp on others. Even though I realize that there is an expected social order of things which says without saying that certain things are acceptable, while other things are not. But I think that we would all agree that many things have changed over the years. In fact very little in our society has survived the wave of time at least when it comes to values. Many of the things that we did yesteryear are but a fleeting memory; some are archived so deep that that they are probably lost forever.

Case in point; Remember when a man would open the car

door for a woman? Remember when he would seat her by pulling out her chair? Remember the days when a man tipped his hat when greeting a woman? And speaking of hats, all men took off their hats when they entered a building. Or how about when a man walked on the curb side of the street to keep his sweetie from harm's way? I don't think that the average person born after the sixties would be familiar with such social pleasantries unless they were witnessed on television or reminisced by a grandparent. Even for me some of those things are long gone, but those things were the order of their day.

Or how about something as simple as holding the door for others, or looking people in the eyes when you speak to them or shake hands? Do our young people even know how to shake hands? Most that I have encountered do not! Shouldn't everyone know how to do these things? I was out at a restaurant eating lunch not long ago and experienced a wonderful thing. A father of five children and his wife were standing in line in front of me when the father noticed me standing behind him. He looked me in my eyes extended his hand, and spoke. As he shook my hand, he instructed his two boys, who were entertaining each other, to do the same. He took care to tell his young boys to look me in the eyes and firmly shake my hand, and guess what? They did exactly as they were instructed, just as their father asked. I think most would agree that even though this was a very basic lesson, most of our kids are not being taught it. In fact, when a young person demonstrates some of these skills, it stands out as abnormal or extraordinary. Why are we so surprised when our kids are polite? When they possess certain social skills? Because it's so rarely demonstrated, that's why, and, when they are, we're in shock.

On the contrary, I was in a grocery store full filling my "honey-do" list when I saw a young who looked to be in is late twenties with a little boy. I can only assume that the little fella was his son who appeared to be about three or four years old. The conversation that they were having caught my attention and took me by surprise. The young man appeared to be teaching the child how to say a phrase; that phrase was, "What's up fool?"

The little boy was doing his best to emulate his instructor as he was being pushed down the aisle in his cart. As this child was learning this phrase from his adult mentor, he was encouraged with high fives when he got it correct and encouraged to repeat it over and over. I wonder what kind of problems this little boy will encounter in life as he grows older with that kind of guidance in his life.

Remember how you dreaded if the principal or teacher had to call home because of something that you did in school? Remember how you felt? How you would do anything to avoid that phone call? It was as if life were about to end. As far as the parents of old were concerned, the teacher's word was bond. If they said you did it (or didn't do it), that was it. When the parents came to the school, they came ready to handle business; they went to set their kids straight and even apologize for their behavior. Somehow that scenario has changed. Now when the child's home is called about his/her behavior or suspension, it is the teacher who is in fear. Now, that mother or guardian is coming to the school not to reprimand or challenge the child about the behavior, she is coming to reprimand and challenge the teacher! Parents will ask, "Why are you picking on my child?" "Why are you kicking him/her out again?" What did you do to my child?" I've seen this more times than I care to mention. On one occasion, I recall arresting the child for assaulting the teacher and lodging him in the juvenile detention center. Then, I had to arrest the parent for attempting to do the same thing and lodge her in the county jail! How things have changed!

How much of that child's behavior is his fault, and how much of it is the mother's? Whose fault is it? Even though we judge the child, is it really his/her fault when the child doesn't know any better? I've been guilty of saying things like, "You should know better." Well, to know better is to do better! I will say that it's my fault, maybe not for the initial violation, but certainly for that which follows. If children don't know any better after leaving my presence, I've done something wrong. You must remember that these young people will grow up to be adults someday and if they aren't taught now, when and how will they

learn? What happens when they have children, and their children have children, who will teach them? Over the years I have
personally made it a point to make sure that every young person
I come in contact with be given some type of instruction and guidance. Remember the young man at the gym? He may not remember the encounter that we had, but at least he had it. He
may not appreciate it or even care, but at least it was given. I've
heard others say that it's not my job to do this or say that, that's
what they have parents for. My question is to those who think
that way, "Whatever happened to the village?" I choose to be my
brother's keeper.

Here is a funny but true story. It is funny in one sense and
sad in another. I'll let you be the judge. I happened to be out at
an event and had to go to the little boys' room. The amusing part
was, as I headed to one of the stalls, I saw a little boy about 6 or
7 years-old standing doing his thing. The funny (or sad) part was
he barely had to pull the pants down to use the bathroom because
they were already half way to his knees when he walked in. The
kids call it "Saggin."

CHAPTER TEN

PULL YOUR PANTS UP

A short story you may or may not find amusing. Of the many things that I do, I work part time at a community college in our town. One day I was assigned to one of our smaller sites which also houses a federally-funded job site, for example, Work First Initiative or Career Alliance. The aim of these institutions is help people get qualified so that they can locate employment locally or abroad. Anyway, I observed an African-American young man who looked to be about 18 or so speaking with one of the job counselors; with the young man was a boy around 5-6 years old. I couldn't help but notice that the young man was wearing jeans that were at best around his lower hip line clearly exposing the crack of his... I mean showing his underwear. I thought to myself, if I were the employer, would I be interested in hiring a person that didn't even know how to wear a pair of pants properly?

Then, I wondered if I should mention this fact to this young man or should I just let it go. Well, I'm ashamed to say that I let it go. I went on with what I was doing, not saying a word. As I walked to the other side of the campus, I regretted not saying anything to the young man. To make myself feel better, I began to rationalize my decision not to say anything to him. After all, who am I to correct everything that I see? Let him learn the hard way; he's old enough to know better. (I can't believe I just said that!)

Anyway, about a half hour had past and I was still thinking maybe I should have said something. While I was sitting in my office, I saw the young man walk by with his half pint buddy. Then, I walked up to him and asked him if he was looking for a job. He seemed surprised by the question but answered, "Yes." I then said, "Wel,l the first thing you need to do is pull your pants up; that may help." He then looked at me as if to say, you guessed it, "You ain't my daddy" and walked off. I knew it! I should've kept my big mouth shut! I read somewhere, "Don't cast your pearls to the swine." Is that what I just did? Cast my pearls to the swine?

After our brief encounter, I went back to my office and replayed the scenario in my mind and thought, "What's the use?" Am I going to challenge every person I see that has his pants around his butt? A small voice said, "No, just that one!" As I was sitting there, a strange thing happened. I saw that same young man walking towards my office. As he got closer, I got up and went to the door and asked him to come in. I introduced myself and asked him his name. He told me his name was Justin and he was seventeen years old, and the little fella with him was his five-year-old brother. Then, I asked him if he thought that I was wrong for telling him to pull his pants up. Justin told me that he thought I was right. He informed me that when he walked away at first he was angry, but the more he thought about it he decided to pull them up. Where was that pearl?

I asked him why he wasn't in school, to which he shared that he didn't finish high school but only had a few classes to complete. I suggested that he go back to school and finish what he started or he would regret it for the rest of his life. He looked at me as if what I had told him was very familiar. Justin then stated, "Yeah, that's what my mom keeps telling me." Then, I asked him where his father was. Justin then disconnected for a moment, looked away and said that his father lived out of town and he doesn't see him much. I told him that he needed to go back to school and finish just like his mother said. He agreed. I told him that when he finished that, keep moving forward. I told him if he were ever at the site, stop by and say hello. Justin said that he would do just that.

While working in the schools, one of the biggest complaints and irritants was the issue with our young boys and girls "Saggin" or wearing their pants around their butts or thighs exposing their underwear. I think all would agree that Saggin is a phenomenon that has certainly outlived its welcome. It has lasted longer than bell bottoms, miniskirts, skinny jeans, and most other styles of dress that have come along and has certainly created more controversy than any other style than I can recall in recent memory. So much so, that some cities have written ordinances banning this form of dress in the public's eye; my city was one of them.

From my recollection, Saggin has been around now for about a decade or so. It is a form of dress that seems to have been made popular by the hip hop/rap culture beginning around the early to mid 90s and, unfortunately, is still alive and well today. It seemed to have started with the oversized pants and evolved from there and appears to have no end in sight for this popular yet socially unacceptable fad. It has been such a craze; it has transcended gender, racial, cultural and even national boundaries.

You can't go into any urban elementary, middle, or high school without seeing the vast majority of students attempting to display their Fruit of the Looms and boxers. I can tell you from experience, with over fifteen years in the Flint school system, that this had been a constant but unwelcomed battle. So much so, that most school districts have written this despicable display into their Student Code of Conduct manuals.

This is not just limited to inner city schools any longer. Affluent and rural schools are now facing the same challenge. This is one reason many districts have gone to school uniforms in an attempt to lay to rest this butt-bearing beast. The thought being that if they could control it at the primary and middle school levels, they could weed it out before the students got to high school where most public schools could not enforce the policy. The sad thing is I have witnessed scores of children suspended from school, forfeiting their precious education for the sake of showing their hind end. To add insult to injury, I have observed many parents who refused to make their children follow the school's uniform policy, willing to sacrifice their education for the right to wear their pants on their butts. I have witnessed many parents who have come up to the schools arguing with teachers and administrators regarding the dress policy. Many of these same parents are the ones who were absent during teacher conferences and report card pick up.

Some say that the exact origin of "Saggin" can be traced back to the Los Angeles County Jail, in the 90s where fresh male inmates that were available for, shall we say, sexual encounters were required to wear their pants low, indicating that they were available. There are some that argue the point, but, whatever the reason or however it came about, the message is still the same. PULL YOU PANTS UP! There are not many things that people agree on these days. We disagree and fight over many issues in this country. We argue over religious issues, political issues, right-to-life issues, racial issues, but there's one issue that we can truly say United we Stand, and that is, PULL YOUR DAD BLAME PANTS UP! It's bad enough for kids to do it, but it's absolutely pathetic to see a 30-, 40-, 50-year-old man walking around showing the crack of his behind.

The sad thing about this is, there is a generation of children who do not know what it feels like to wear their pants around their waists. While working in the schools, it was a daily ritual for me to tell the students to pull up their pants. Many would respond, by telling me they were already up. Many kids honestly thought that if their pants were around their lower hip line they were up. In the past years, this "Naggin Saggin" has even become popular with some of our young ladies. Not only do we see boys walking around showing off their boxer drawers, we now see girls walking around holding their pants up while they waddle down the street like slue foot ducks.

I was in one of our local markets not long ago. As I was walking past one of the aisles, what I saw caused me to back up and take a closer look. I saw a child about 2-3 years old with big baggie Saggin pants, an oversized shirt, and a ball cap turned to the side. Oh, did I mention that he had an earring in his ear? The strange thing was that he looked at *me* as if I were an alien! Now of course, the child didn't know any better, but some might agree that he was certainly being set up for failure. I had to catch myself staring at this pint-sized baby thug, because his mother caught me staring with my mouth open looking at her child who was a mini-version of a rapper if I ever say one. She grabbed the boy by his arm, and said, "bring yo a** on" and dragged the boy off to the next aisle, and out of sight. Is it me? Or is it something wrong with that picture.

WHERE IS ADAM?

There are not many funny thing that we experience as police officers. But one that sticks out in my memory, was when I got into a foot chase with two boys that had stolen a car. Now I must mention that the car theft in of itself wasn't funny. The part was, when they got out of the car to run from me, I didn't have to run very fast to catch them. You see, chasing people who have their pants around their knees is not much of a challenge, even for an old guy like me. Well, I guess Saggin isn't so   bad   after   all.

CHAPTER ELEVEN

A MOTHER'S LOVE
(Hi, Mom!)

Here's a familiar scene. A celebrity or athlete is in front of the camera for whatever reason. What is the first thing that comes out of his/her mouth? Is it "Hey, Dad"? No! It's "Hey, Mom" or "I love you, Mom." Fellas don't hate. That's just the way it is. It doesn't matter if you've been there from the beginning. It doesn't matter if you taught them everything they know; don't expect any air time. It just ain't going to happen. I know it sounds like I'm envious, but can we get a shout out sometime??? Ok, can you at least say "Hey, Mom and Dad?" Truth be told mothers deserve all that and more; don't you think?

It has been said that there is nothing like a mother's love. When everyone else gives up and throws in the towel, a mother's love will endure until the end. She will go through hell and high water for her children. Don't you ever try and come between a mother and her children; you are likely to suffer great bodily injury. She will willingly sacrifice her own comfort and well being to provide for them, even if it means risking her very life. A mother's love transcends logic. When it seems certain that that son or daughter has lost all sense of reality and has crossed the line of life and appears never to return, a mother will remain hopeful, and, in many cases, prayerful that her children, no matter how old they are or how far they've gone, will somehow miraculously regain their senses. When father washes his hands and says that's it, a mother's love is just getting started; wouldn't you agree? Thank God for a mother's love, for without it many of us would have been lost and hung out to dry a long time ago. I'm reminded of the many years as a police officer on the unforgiving streets of Flint when I would get domestic calls to homes where adult children who were in their 30s, 40s, and even 50s were abusing their parents. If there happened to be fathers in the homes, they would tell me that they had washed their hands of their now adult children a long time ago. But their wives— the mothers of these still adolescent-behaving adults—were still helping them, still feeding them, still clothing them, still defending them, even when they were abused by their adult children who should have been long gone.

I've seen on many occasions where these adult children have even assaulted and battered their parents, maybe the funds were cut off, or the parents had had enough and the children were asked to leave. I recall on one occasion that I was sent by the dispatcher to a family dispute. When I arrived I found that it was a mother of about 70 years old who called about her son who was out of control. I soon found out that her son was about 20 years older than I at the time. Here you have a 30-year-old police officer telling a 50-year-old man that he needed to grow up. Was there something wrong with that picture? There were situations where adult children were asked to leave but refused because they had nowhere to go. I remember one call in particular that I was sent to a home for another family dispute, only to find that the argument was about a 30 year-old who refused to wash dishes!???? You know what I did to solve the problem? I went into the kitchen, washed the dishes, and made him dry. I told the members of that family that if I got a call back to the house someone was going to jail. Looking back, I don't know who the bigger fool was—me for washing the dishes or the mother for calling. Needless to say, in my younger days, I would do just about anything to keep the peace. Oh, by the way, they got the message, and I didn't get a call back to the house.

I've known people who have older adult children who

have substance abuse problems who would regularly steal from their parents. The fathers would be ready to grab the shotgun while the mothers would leave the door unlocked for them so that they wouldn't have to damage it when they came back to steal more. Their logic being, if they were going to come in, the door may as well be unlocked so they didn't have to kick it in. A mother's love is something hard to explain. Thank God for them. As with most things, there is an upside and a downside. The downside to that same love is when one doesn't know when to step back and let nature take its course, not knowing when to help our children up and when to let them get up on their own. There is wisdom in knowing and understanding that tough love is love, too. I will use a couple personal examples of what I mean by tough love.

CHAPTER TWELVE

A FATHER'S LOVE
(It's Time To Fly)

If you remember, I shared that I have twins, Quion and Quiana, and, by the time you read this book, they will have celebrated their 21st birthday. I'm very proud of my children, and I regularly tell them that. When my son turned 19, I told him that I was giving him a few more months and I was cutting him off from paying his cell phone bill. At 20, my daughter was given that same notice. Well, my wife, his mother, was not very keen on the idea at first. She felt that our son was a starving college student and had little extra money to work with. He still needed our help and she ended her statements with an "after all he's a good kid." Can I clarify something; both of my kids stay at home and eat my food while they attend college, so ain't no starvation goin' in my crib. And he's supposed to be good. That's the way we raised him. To be more accurate, he's not a good kid; he's a good young adult.

You see, my attitude changed when I counted over 10 pair of expensive tennis shoes which were valued from $70-$150 lined up in my son's bedroom with matching ball caps, that ranged from $25 and up each (that I didn't buy I might add). When I saw old tennis shoes in the garage used for cutting the grass that were nicer than the ones I wore every day, I decided it was time. Time to fly, time to cut him off, what do you think!?? That mother's love that we appreciated so much in the first half of this chapter has now taken on a different characteristic, a different look if you will.

Let me share a story or two with you. A couple of years ago during one of our typical Michigan winters, we had about 12-15 inches of snow blow through one evening. When we went to bed that night, we had about three inches on the ground. When we woke up, there was well over a foot on the ground. It was actually quite beautiful if you like snow. One of Quion's responsibilities is to make sure that the driveway, porch, and sidewalks are salted and clear. Of course, I do my fair share of snow removal, but the job is primarily his.

On this particular snowy day, I woke my son up and suggested that he grab the old snow blower and go out and make some money because there was plenty to be made. Needless to say, he got dressed, grabbed the blower and a shovel along with the keys to my GMC Denali, and off he went in the wild white yonder. I was so proud of my son. He was out making his own money; he was learning to be independent. That meant that he could get out of my pocket for a minute, maybe even pay his own phone bill for a month or two (that's kind of selfish, isn't it?). Anyway, Quion was gone all day. For at least six hours he was out in the cold working and learning to make his own way. Of course, his mother asked me on more than one occasion if I should call him and see if he were hungry. I assured her that if he were hungry or thirsty or had to use the bathroom, he surely could do those things without her assistance. The first part was a mother's love; the second part was a father's love. Needless to say, Ms. Wheeler didn't appreciate my sarcasm and continued to cook, a meal that had filled the house with a great aroma and had lightly steamed the kitchen windows.

I don't know to this day if his mother called him, but somehow it was as if Quion had smelled the food that was cooking because he returned. Just as the meal was ready to be served, with perfect timing, he returned home, cold, tired, and ready to eat. He kicked off his wet boots in the heated breeze way and took off his wet gloves. I saw that he was beaming from ear to ear with the money he had earned. He seemed really proud of himself for braving the cold and deep snow and making a mound of money.

I wasn't as happy as he was, however. You see, before he left, he didn't take the time to shovel his own driveway. He was so focused on making money that he forgot that our driveway needed to be shoveled as well. Helping others is something that I've always taught my children. But I've also stressed that before you go off and do something for someone else, you make sure that your family is taken care of first. You never do for someone else before you do for your own house. Unfortunately, Quion forgot that lesson as he headed off that early morning on his shoveling expedition. Because he had neglected to shovel the snow in his own driveway, his mother and I had gotten stuck trying to get in and out because he had the truck. On a couple of occasions, I had to push his mother out of the driveway because it was so full of snow.

What I told him next was sure to be met with opposition from my loving wife. I told him to get dressed, go outside, and take care of his responsibility. This took him totally by surprise. He looked at me and said, "But, Dad, I'm tired from working all day." I then gave him the look. You know the look, don't you? It is that he look that says, "boy, if you don't do what I just told you, I'm gonna..." You know—that look! He got the message and grabbed a fresh jacket, a fresh pair of boots and gloves, and went to work the driveway. As he was heading out the door, I poured a little salt into the wound by telling him that if he would have shoveled before he left the house this morning when the snow was light and fluffy, it probably would have only taken about 15-20 minutes. But because we had been in and out of the driveway all day, the snow had packed down and now had ruts in it, making it much more difficult, it was probably going to take at least an hour or two. I told him not to stop until the job was completed.

I was tempted to go out and help, but felt that it was a lesson he had to learn. I noticed that as he was shoveling I could see his attitude with every scoop of snow. It was as if he were talking as he shoveled. I could almost hear him. Who... (scoop) does he, think...(scoop) he is... (scoop) making... me shovel... (scoop) he could have... done this...while...I was...gone (scoop). Well, as you would have it, Ms. Wheeler, his dear mother, told me that I was too hard on the boy, that I should let him do it in the morning, and let him come in and eat.

As lovingly as I could, I told my dear wife, and I quote, "You be the mother, and I'll be the father." My son will learn this lesson tonight, not tomorrow! That didn't set too well with her at the time, but since then she has learned to appreciate my perspective and input as a father. Well, after about an hour and a half, Quion was finally finished, and a great job he did. He came into the house huffing, puffing, and starving; you would have thought that he hadn't eaten in a week. He didn't say much at dinner or for the rest of the evening. I don't know if he were too angry or too tired to talk, but he showered and went straight to bed. He deserved a good night's rest. Once again I was proud of my son.

The next day he approached me and said, "Dad, I got the lesson. I should always take care of family first!" We hugged, and that was the last time this was mentioned until now. I've had to teach other hard lessons, but that one was understood without a doubt. So, when he is supposed to cut the grass, he cuts it. When he is supposed to take out the garbage, he takes it out. When he is supposed to do the other things that he is responsible for, he does it! And he does it well. He's been trained to do those things. He's been given an example of how to do them; he's been given opportunity to do them. Now, he simply does what he's supposed to do.

If you will indulge me for a moment, I have another story. As you know from my bio, I am the owner and Chief Instructor of Double Dragon Karate School. We have an outstanding staff of Black Belt instructors and instructor trainees; some are as young as 12 years old.

We have a pretty tough requirement at our school for our Black belts. Before you can wear your Black belt, you must complete at least 100 hours of assisted training. The reason being, we want our Black belts to be competent, confident, and capable before they strap their belts around their waists. I believe we are probably the only school in the area that has such stringent requirements which is above and beyond the actual Black belt physical and written tests which is a challenge within itself. I believe that is why we have multiple Local, Regional, and International Champions at our school.

The tradition hasn't always been met with raving approval. Case in point: I actually had a mother call me and give a laundry list of things that *I* should be doing to ensure that her teenage son is allowed to wear his Black belt. It was a belt that he successfully tested for two months prior. In so many words, I was told that I wasn't doing enough for him. I was given many suggestions to help this 14-year-old young man fulfill his commitments. She said that I wasn't doing this, and maybe I should be doing that. It was even suggested that a special meeting be held with her son in an attempt to motivate him to do the things that everyone else that has come before him has done without issue. She felt that maybe he wasn't sure of what was required of him even if everyone else did. Mind you he was but one of about a dozen and a half Black belts ranging from the age of 12-55 that had somehow managed to fulfill their requirements, but for some reason her son needed special attention.

Now, don't get me wrong. I'm not opposed to helping my students when I see that they are in need of help; as a matter of fact, it's my responsibility. But when you are mentally and physically capable of the task set before you and you choose not to do the things that are required of you, well, that's on you.

Allow me to say that this young fellow is not a bad kid, nor does he have bad parents. Quite the contrary, they are an awesome family. But this is a perfect example of a mother's love gone wild, a love that stifles and chokes out necessary growth. Oh, did I mention that during our conversation, the mother actually (jokingly I hope) offered to buy service hours just so her son could wear his belt like the other students? Now, I don't know how you feel about that, but I told her that what she jokingly suggested was not going to happen. Her son had to fulfill his commitment like everyone else with no exceptions.

Later that day the young man came to class. At the end of the session, announcements and instructions were given on the schools upcoming events, I noticed that after class he went outside and spoke to his mother who was waiting in the car. Moments later she came into the school and asked me for the same updates on the upcoming activities that I had just announced in-class. She informed me that the information never made it to her. Then, I kindly grabbed her by the hand and walked her to my office where I explained to her that she needed to stop handicapping her son. I told her that he was old enough to pay attention; he was also old enough to handle the responsibility of relaying simple information. Also, I told her that if she wanted to help her son, she didn't need to buy his way; she didn't need to follow behind him like he was 6-years-old. I continued by saying that what she needed to do was impress upon him the importance of taking responsibility and getting serious about his responsibilities. Then, I told her that any future information would have to be forwarded to her by her son.

After I gave her this mild tongue lashing, I braced myself for retaliation. I waited for a front punch or back kick or something violent, but it never came. Instead, she graciously said, "You're right!" I don't know if she meant it or if she were making plans to get me in the parking lot when I closed the school. However, I think she actually got the message. To be totally honest, I was actually expecting them to quit, but, as for the moment, they are still with us. The son now comes to me with questions pertaining to his development, not his mother.

Now, we know that all of our mothers are not guilty of "over loving" their children, but many have unintentionally ruined their boys (and girls), handicapping, and even denying them the growth opportunities that come from these important life lessons. These are lessons that they will most certainly need if they hope to grow and develop into strong, responsible, capable young men and women. Our young people must learn that there are things in life that you can't beg, borrow, or steal; they must be earned! They must understand the principle of being committed to the things that are important and enduring until the task has been completed. Why would we cheat them of that lesson?

If I could use an example of the butterfly as a comparison, I learned that this creature has four stages of development: the egg, the larva or caterpillar stage, the pupa or chrysalis stage, and, finally, the beautiful butterfly. Also, I discovered that the entire growth process is accomplished only during the larva stage, not the pupa or butterfly stage. In my mind's eye, this is equivalent to the fundamental and developmental years of a child, where what they are exposed to and taught will be crucial for their development and success in life. If they are robbed of this critical opportunity, in many cases (not all), they will not become what they were destined to be.

The other important and final stage of the butterfly is what is called, "hatching." During hatching, the pupa forces and pushes within its cocoon or case until it splits. It struggles and fights to break free from its cocooned state until it is freed. This takes quite a bit of time and effort, but it must be done. Once freed, its body, which is filled with fluid, instinctively begins to pump that fluid into its waiting withered wings. Once the fluid is pumped, the wings come to life and become *functional*. The process is not over until the wings are dried in the sun. Then and only then, will the butterfly be able to take to the sky as it was intended filling the world with its beauty.

Imagine if you will if someone interrupted this necessary process after watching the struggle of the soon-to-be butterfly. If anyone assisted the butterfly instead of allowing it to do its own pushing, its own fighting, and its own straining to break free from its case, a person with good intention would unknowingly think that s/he would be doing this creature a favor by rescuing it from a necessary process that was detrimental to its very survival. And s/he would, without question, contribute to not only preventing it from becoming what it was destined to be, but giving it a certain death sentence.

You see, the struggle and the strain is a process of life for the butterfly. Without it, it would not be able to break free. Without it, it would not be able to have strength in its wings to fly, and, without it, it would be functionless. Oh! Also, I learned that some species of butterflies fly over two thousand miles to warmer climates. So, let's teach our children to fly, not carry them on our backs.

CHAPTER THIRTEEN

WAIT UNTIL YOUR FATHER GETS HOME

I was sharing the idea of this book with another friend named Derrick. As Derrick and I were reminiscing and talking about this book, we reflected on how time has seemed to fly by. We began to laugh about the "good old days", and he mentioned an experience he had growing up. He shared with me the time he and his neighborhood buddies were playing football in the front yard. He shared that his mother told him to stay out of the neighbor's yards while they were playing. He told me that he took his mother's instruction with a grain of salt because the game was going too well to stop. He and his buddies were having a great time, and, besides, his father was not at home, so he knew he had a few more downs to play. So he ignored his mother's directives to stay out of the neighbor's yard and they continued to have a grand old time as he and his best buddies trampled not only his lawn which was a no-no, but the lawn of at least two of his neighbors, which was a bigger no-no.

Derrick shared that a strange thing happened in the middle of one of their biggest plays; as he was going deep for the big one, he saw his father's car coming down the street. His heart began to race as he saw his father pull into the driveway in what seemed like slow motion. As his dad got out of the car, he watched as his mother talked with him and pointed in his direction. Even though he couldn't hear a word of their conversation, he knew they were talking about him. That conversation seemed to last forever, as they would occasionally look in his direction. He thought he saw his father's eyes turn red as he glared in his direction, which sent chills through his spine.

Derrick thought he would find temporary comfort as he looked for support and strength from his best buddies that he just risked his life for, but, when he turned around, they were nowhere to be found. The only thing left of their game was the football that had now rested in the neighbor's yard—the yard he was told to stay out of. Derrick said that he broke out in a cold sweat as his parents continued to talk.

What came next was confirmation of the conversation, and he felt a knawing in the pit of his stomach. He instantly remembered the short directive given by his mother, "STAY OUT OF THE NEIGHBOR'S YARD!" The next thing was his father moving at the speed of an all Pro NFL linebacker charging a second string high school quarterback. Should he run, if only he could move his feet which seemed to be cemented to the ground. Before he could turn and escape, his middle-aged father had covered not only the length of his front yard, but the neighbor's yard as well. The only thing he could remember were repetitious whacks to his rear end in syllables...Why...Didn't... You...Listen...To...Your...Mother...When...She...Told...You...To...Stay...Out...Of...The...Neighbor's...Yard! Yep, his dad tanned his butt real good that day. Looking back Derrick said that he deserved it; he should have listened to his mother. He added that he remembered hearing his mother threaten him with the wrath of his father from time to time. Derrick was also quick to share that it was that influence that kept him out of prison and on the straight and narrow.

Nick, another friend of mine, shared a story with me when he was a kid growing up. Nick lived with his parents and older brother. They lived at the end of the block in what we call a cul-de-sac. He said that they had a gravel driveway and his mother was always telling them not to throw rocks because they were going to break someone's window. Like most boys, Nick ignored his mother's instructions and continued throwing rocks across the street. Well, on one particular day, Nick decided that once again he was going to throw rocks while his mother wasn't looking. But this day was different; Nick said he found a beauty of a rock that seemed to beg him to be thrown. He picked it up, looked to see if anyone were looking and chucked it across the street, feeling pretty good about himself. No lightning had fallen. No thunder rolled and he was safe once again, or so he thought. He had thrown many rocks in his day, possibly hundreds without incident, but unbeknownst to him, somehow this special rock had gained enough velocity that it flew clear across the street and into back window of the neighbor's Volkswagen Rabbit. Crash!!!! In today's texting vernacular the response would be OMG!!!!

Well, needless to say, Nick instantly regained his memory and could now clearly hear his mother's voice as clear as a bell ("Boy, you better stop throwing them rocks before you break something."). He then sought asylum in his bedroom, hoping somehow what he had just experienced was just a bad dream. He wished that he could somehow start the day all over again, this time taking heed to his mother's request and ignoring the shiny rock that was calling his name. While Nick was in his delusional state, he heard a loud knock at the front door, a knock that was determined to get the attention of anyone that may be in the house. He heard his mother answer the door followed by a muffled conversation. He thought he recognized the voice to be that of his neighbor and owner of the Volkswagen Rabbit that was now missing a rear window, if somehow he could just disappear. He looked for an escape route but found none. He was trapped!

After the conversation ended, the neighbor left, and his mother went about what she was doing prior to his stopping by. What had just happened? Did they just exchange recipes? Were they talking politics? What?! His mother didn't say anything; the suspense was killing him. Maybe it was just a dream. Was it safe to come out of the room? Well, after much deliberation he decided to venture out of his room where he saw his mother standing with her hands on her hips (not a good sign) and had this strange look on her face, a look that he had seen before. She only had to say one thing, and that was: *Your father will deal with you when you he gets home.* It was as if the blood drained from his body; he couldn't think. He couldn't see straight. It was as if the world stopped moving. The hours that followed were unbearable. Nick swore he could hear every car door slam in the neighborhood. The waiting was worse than any punishment that he could experience. If there were such a thing as 911 back then, he would have certainly called them to rescue him. And then it happened. His father came home. It didn't take long for his dad to be filled in with the day's events. What happened next was what Nick described as a redefining moment in his young life. From that point on, what his mother said was golden. Yes, his father handled it.

Remember when mom was the nurturer and dad was the disciplinarian? He was called in only when things got totally out of control. Mom would do the best she could, but she always had an option, and that option was dad. She could pull dad out of her skirt and use him like Zorro used his sword. The very mention of his name would convince or coerce good behavior. It was not that mom was weak; we just knew that dad meant business!

She could hold his title over the kid's head like an ax to regain compliance and civility when her children would have their moments of temporary insanity. So when all else failed, when all other methods had been exhausted, Mom could make the ultimate statement, the ultimate threat if you will, and that was, WAIT UNTIL YOUR FATHER GETS HOME. "Wait until your father gets home" were words that no child wanted to hear. It invoked fear and terror in the hearts of children everywhere. They would break out into uncontrolled fits, shake and shiver, and cry uncontrollably. You know the cry I'm talking about. You would huff and puff and couldn't catch your breath while trying to talk.

Yes. "Wait until your father gets home" would solve absolutely every and any problem that could ever exist. I was speaking with a coworker who shared with me that she had one son in particular that she had a hard time getting through to. She shared that when she ran out of options she would simply say,

"Your father will deal with you when he gets home." And you know what? He did, and it worked.

But a strange thing has happened over the years. Fewer and fewer mothers have this option. The reason? Fathers aren't coming home as they once did because fewer and fewer fathers are around. A large number of today's children don't see a father coming through the door. Many don't even have a male role model to look up to. This is certainly due to the great numbers of their fathers, uncles, and older brothers that are not in their lives because they are unknown, absent, dead, or incarcerated.

On that topic, the incarceration rate is at an all time high in our country, with more men entering the prison system than ever before. And, to add insult to injury, more and more women are being incarcerated, many of these women being mothers. When you break it down racially, the rate is disproportionately higher in the African-American and Hispanic or Latino communities given their populations or 13 and 15 percent respectively. There are some studies that suggest that there are more African-American men in prison than in college. Why is this happening? Is this just exclusive to this particular race of people? We know that is not true because the Hispanic population has its fair share of social ills as well, as do other minority races in this country. How do Caucasians and other races fit into this category?

The question is why—why is this tragedy and phenomenon going on? The more important questions to ask is: What is happening to all the children of these incarcerated and absenteeparents? Who's minding the store? Who's taking care of the kids? Who's going to the parent-teacher conferences? Who's taking them to their basketball games, their soccer and karate practices, and dance recitals? Who's going over the home work? Who's taking care of our kids?

One day not long ago, I had a very familiar conversation with a young man that was brought into the police department, a conversation that I have had with literally hundreds of young men over the years. This particular young man was under arrest for trespassing and fleeing and eluding (running from the police). He had been with some other boys, one of which was in possession of a gun. This young man was like hundreds of other young men that I have come in contact with and spoken to throughout my twenty-three year career as a police officer. When I asked him why he wasn't in school, he gave me the typical answer stating that he didn't know. He was currently enrolled in an alternative school within the district, but decided to skip school and hang out at another school with some of his buddies who were in the same boat as he. When asked why he had to attend the alternative school, he told me it was because he was kicked out of the regular school because...you guessed it; he frequently skipped, got into trouble, and his grades were very poor.

He shared with me that he lived with his mother and that she was doing the best that she could, but he just couldn't keep it together. I asked him the question of the ages; a question that I have asked every child that I have come into contact with that was arrested, and that was, "Where is your father?" He shared with me that even though his father was in town, he was not in his life. I told him that that was too bad, but I also shared with him that he could still go on to do great things if he changed his friends and readjusted his focus. I then told this young man that I had a son about his age and told him that my son was no better than he was. I asked this young man, who was headed to court for the third of fourth time, what he thought was the difference between him and my son. With his head hanging like a defeated fighter, he responded, "Your son has you." I don't know if that young man knew how important the words were that he just said. But I certainly did.

While he and I were having this conversation, there happened to be a female officer in an adjoining office listening to our conversation. She later shared with me that she overheard the conversation I had with this kid and she told me that she couldn't come out the office because she was so overwhelmed with emotion. Having the same passion as I did for our young people, she and I talked for a while about the enormity of the problems facing our young people, especially our boys. Even though this officer and I worked in the same division, doing the same job, she expressed her frustration with me about how she is constantly trying to reach these young men. I must say that I have great respect for this officer and the tremendous passion she possesses for children.

At the end of the day, I reflected on that conversation that I had with that young man. I remember what he said, "Your son has you." Yes, my son does have me but that's a two-way street because I can also say that I am proud that I have him as well. We have each other. Isn't that the way it's supposed to be? I know that that's not the way it is in many cases, but that is the way it's supposed to be.

I shared with him that if he didn't make better choices, that if he didn't change his direction and associations, he was going to either end up dead or in jail. Those seemed to be familiar words to him. I can imagine that he's been told this a time or two in his short life, perhaps by his mother, or another relative. While he was being fingerprinted and prepared for court by the arresting officer, I wanted to make sure I left him with something positive. I told him that he could do it, that he could make it if he put his mind to it. In a somber tone, he acknowledged my attempts to encourage him by saying, "Yes, Sir." I don't know if he got it. I don't know if he even believed that he could do it. I can only hope that he finds the strength to fight through his many challenges. It is only a matter of choice, isn't it?

If he doesn't and fails, he won't be the first to do so. If he does and finds success, I'm confident that he won't be the last. As for me, I'll keep trying. I'll keep talking and planting seeds, maybe one of them will take root and germinate and grow into something special. Like the young lady I mentioned earlier, this young man has also been cheated—cheated from truly knowing how great he is and can be, cheated from the love and guidance from his father. But you know what? Perhaps, his father was cheated as well. I have a feeling that "wait until your father gets home" is something that this young man has never heard. I've discovered something along the way: Growth does not rest solely in one person's hands. Development depends on many sources. Let's make a deal. If you plant the seed, I promise to water it for you.

CHAPTER FOURTEEN HOW

THINGS HAVE CHANGED
(The Good Ol' Days)

A famous song performed by over 50 artists sets up this chapter. It is the song, "Everything Must Change," a song that lets us know that change is inevitable. Most of us can appreciate the changes we have witnessed and experienced in our lifetime, especially in the areas of automobile design, medicine, technology, and science. I think that most would agree that those changes have been much needed and welcomed. But there are other areas where change has not been so welcomed, but somehow it occurred just the same.

I'm not that old (well, maybe I am) but I remember when there was only one television in the house and it was in the family or living room. I also recall that after the news, that was pretty much all she wrote, the "boob tube," as we used to call it, was done for the night. There was no late night TV, and there weren't 450 channels to keep you up all night. The Air Force jets went across the screen; the flag waved. That was it, lights out. I remember in the 70s our neighbor had channel 100, and we used to sneak and watch it when his parents were at work. Now, it did not have 100 channels. It was just called "Channel 100." Look at us now.

I was talking to a 14-year-old young man the other day who was admiring my iPad 2 while I was sitting in the local book store. He mentioned that he was going to ask his mom to get him one for his upcoming birthday. Seeing that an iPad 2 can set you back well over $600, I told him that that was going to be some kind of birthday gift. He shrugged his shoulders and asked me how many songs, books, and games applications I had on my iPad? When I told him I had about 1500 songs, several books, and about 10 games on it, he didn't seem impressed. I then had to take this young man down memory lane to show him how impressive my library really was, especially when you consider that I had all of that contained in something as small as an envelope. These kids have no idea, do they!?

I told this young man (we'll call him "Junior") that back in the day we had 8-tracks and albums, 33s and 45s. It wasn't until the mid to late 70s that we had cassette tapes. He then interrupted me and said, "Oh! I've seen one of them once." Junior then asked me how old CDs were. I told him they didn't hit the scene until the mid-80s. Once again Junior didn't seem to be the least impressed. He then told me he heard of albums, but he never heard of an 8-track. He asked me could I fit the 1500 songs I had on my Ipad on one of those??? I told him that about 8 songs would fit on one 8 track. Now, I knew I had his curiosity! I told him if he wanted 1,500 songs on an 8-track he would need to get his mother's minivan, take out the seats, <u>AND</u> get a trailer. I think he got the picture because he raised his eyebrows and rubbed his chin in deep thought. I had to let Junior know that he wasn't nearly as smart as he thought he was. He then said with great confidence and conviction, "I know what a 45 is because my brother got arrested by the police with one, but what is a 33?" While you're laughing, I know you think I made that up, but it's true.

There was a time in our culture that the father was the main breadwinner and the mother stayed home and raised the children. The father went out and got the bacon and the mother fried it up in the pan. There was a time when mom would stand on the porch wearing her apron and wave goodbye as dad backed out the driveway and headed off to work. This may be foreign to some, but I'm sure there are some of you who can actually remember those days.

Unlike *my* household where there are actually more cars than drivers, there was only one car back in those days. Dad used it to go to work as mom cared for the home, went to the school events, and PTA meetings. There were no latch key programs, no federally-funded after school programs, no baby sitters, or day care centers. Mom saw the kids off to school, and she welcomed them when they returned home. Dinner was ready by five or six in the evening when dad returned home from work. Everyone sat at the table together and shared not only a hot meal but also conversation of the day's events. Do you remember those days?

During those days, families got together at one time. And that was at the dinner table. There they shared and caught up on the day's events. But it seems we're letting pressures from our work and school lives get in the way. After all that occurs during a day at school and work, sitting around the dinner table means you get some time to have some real quality time as a family. Unfortunately, this is happening less and less as our society seems to have so much packed in a day.

A study by Fiona Johnston revealed that long working hours were blamed by most, with 40 percent admitting that shifts and late nights in the office meant missing out on a family dinner. Another 36 percent said the family all eat at different times, while 16 percent even said they wanted to watch something on the TV instead of sitting down together. But researchers also found that just *half* of families have their evening meal at the dinner table with more than a *third* saying they are more likely to eat it on the sofa or in front of the TV. Almost *one in twenty* people even said the family members all eat their meal in different parts of the house. Despite this, 94 pe cent of people reckon the evening meal is a great time for families to catch up together. And almost three quarters want to make more effort to get their family sitting down for dinner together.

My how things have changed. The sad part is my family is no different; I have to fight to make everyone sit at the dinner table together. But it is a fight worth having.

CHAPTER FIFTEEN

LET'S TAKE TIME
FOR A
A LITTLE REVIEW

In 1960 a gallon of gas was 25 cents, and by 1969 was 35 cents. When I was in high school in the 70s, it was 55 cents. Today, it's over $3.50, and we're told that it may hit 5 dollars by the summer of 2012. In 1960 the average cost of a new car was $2,600.00 and by 1969 was $3,270.00. Today a new Impala costs over $20,000 and a Cadillac will set you back $38-$65,000 depending on which model you buy.

Days were much simpler back then, days before the Internet, pagers, cell phones, i-Pods, CDs DVDs, Mp3s, and Wiis. Then, the divorce rate wasn't quite so high, where many if not most of your neighbors were two-parent families. You could go next door and borrow a cup of sugar, and your neighbors knew each other, looked out for each other, and, yes, even corrected and disciplined each other's kids without fear of being disrespected or worse. Remember those days? And speaking of the divorce rate, two-parent families are growing scarcer according to a U.S. Study November 24, 1999, University of Chicago.

The traditional U.S. household comprised of a married couple with children has become scarcer, a reflection of more women working and a view that marriage is not always desirable, researchers said. The most common living arrangement in the United States consists of unmarried people and no children, which made up one-third of all households in 1998, double the percentage in 1972.

Meanwhile, the traditional nuclear family, a married couple with children, made up 26 percent of households in 1998, down from 45 percent in 1972, according to a survey conducted by the National Opinion Research Center at the University of Chicago. Timothy Smith, director of the survey, attributed the trend to more women in the work force, driven there by economic necessity and a desire for a career, and a relaxation of social mores that frowned on cohabitation and on having children outside of marriage.

"Marriage has declined as the central institution under which households are organized and children are raised," Smith said, noting the survey found that 62 percent of working-class adults reported being married in the 1994-98 period, down from 80 percent in the 1972-77 period. "People marry later and divorce and cohabitate more. A growing proportion of children has been born outside of marriage. Even within marriage the changes have been profound as more and more women have entered the labor force and gender roles have become more homogenous between husbands and wives," Smith said.

Both parents have jobs in two-thirds of families, compared to just one-third in 1972, the survey found. The percentage of households in which women worked while their husbands stayed at home rose to 4 percent in the 1990s from 2 percent in the 1970s. About half of children now live in a household with their original parents, down from nearly three-quarters of children living in such households in 1972.

Children are born into more single-parent homes than I can recall in recent memory. I must say again I am not attempting to suggest that strong young men and women cannot come from single parent homes raised by mothers and grandmothers. I'm not saying that they cannot go on to do great things and live normal lives; that is not the intent of the book. We all know of countless individuals that have gone on to make incredible strides in the world. They have gone on to be great athletes, entertainers, business owners, politicians, and even presidents. I think we can all agree upon that fact. But my career, my business, my church ministry, and the many years serving and being active in my community have revealed a need to address this very vital issue.

Natalie Low, Ph.D., a clinical psychologist and instructor at Harvard, counsels families as they navigate their way through the illusions and into the reality of marriage. She says the couples she sees are trying to nurture their relationships along with raising perfect kids and maintaining careers, but, in this compartmentalized era, they are without the benefit of support systems of extended families and communities. Couples also expect to be happy. But "the facts of life are very grinding, so the reality of marriage is grinding," says Low, who has been married for 51 years. Marriage is now, as it has always been, hard work. Marriage is not a static event that can be measured, but a series of developments—those triumphs and setbacks—that make up life. "There is no obvious course to follow, so couples just have to keep working. A person sees dramatic changes during a marriage," Low says, "so a couple has to be committed to a way of life.

CHAPTER SIXTEEN

HERE WE GO AGAIN

I don't claim to be the sharpest knife in the drawer, but there's something that I have noticed in the years spent as a School Recourse Officer, something that seemed a bit out of sorts if you will. It didn't matter if I were called to one of the twenty or so elementary schools for which I was responsible. Or one of the middle or high schools that I was assigned to, the observation was the same; where were the parents?

Whenever there was an occasion for me to call the home of a student because of a problem or concern, they were not there. Or as it has happened more times than I care to mention, when the unfortunate situation arose, I had to arrest a student. There seemed to be as many grandparents answering the phone and responding to the police department than mothers and fathers. This growing phenomenon used to puzzle me when I was new on the job. But as time went by, I began to see that this was not the exception; it was fast becoming more of the rule. I also noticed that there were more and more aunts and older siblings coming to see about these troubled children.

On one occasion I recall I had to arrest a 7th grade student for assaulting his teacher. He was taken to the police station where he was processed for assault and battery, a crime which required him to be suspended from the Flint Public Schools for up to 180 days. What was surprising was the person that re-sponded to my call was not a grandparent, not even an aunt or uncle, but an older sister. This young man was being raised by his 21 year-old sister! The interesting thing was, when she ar-rived to the station, it was obvious that she was young, until she began to speak. When she spoke it was apparent that she had been in the parenting role for some time. The maturity and wis-dom that she possessed was not that of an average 21 year-old. She scolded that young man so well it would have made a judge proud. She apologized for his behavior and shared that she had been working with his anger issues for a while.

It was obvious that this young lady hadn't had much time to be a kid because she was too busy being a mother to her brother, who was not much younger than she. When asked where their parents were, she informed me that mother was in jail and she and her brother didn't know who their father was. She shared with me that her mother told her that the father was a "no good so and so." This young woman shared that she attended a local college during the day and took care of her brother while her mother was often in and out of jail. Someone once shared with me that a bad father was better than no father at all. Whether or not you subscribe to that theory is not really the point. People do change, and, at least if there were one, the pos-sibility exists that their lives and circumstances could have been different if there were a father in the picture. If there were a choice between a good one and a bad one; it's my guess they would probably choose a good one. Wouldn't you?

CHAPTER SEVENTEEN

GRANDPARENTS
&
GRANDCHILDREN

In the most recent Census Bureau statistics, there are 74.5 million children ages 0-17 in the United States. There are 3.9 million (6 percent) children in the United States living in a grandparent's home, up 76 percent from the 2.2 million (3 percent) who did so in 1970.

Of the grandparents who maintain homes for their grandchildren, 55 percent of grandmothers and 47 percent of grandfathers are not yet age 55. Additionally, 19 percent of grandmothers and 15 percent of grandfathers are under age 45. About two-thirds of grandparent-maintained families include one or both of the children's parents.

Among grandparent-maintained families, the average household income ranges from $19,750 for those with only a grandmother present to $61,632 for families with both grandparents and at least one of the grandchildren's parents present. Among children in grandparent-headed families, 47 percent live with both grandparents; 47 percent reside with only their grandmother; and 6 percent live with only their grandfather. About two-thirds of these children also reside with at least one of their parents.

Of the children living in a grandparent's home, 42 percent are white; 36 percent are African American; 17 percent are Hispanic. 5 percent are Asian or Pacific Islander or American Indian or Alaska Native.

About 670,000 children across the United States live in their grandmother's home with neither their grandfather nor their parents present. About two-thirds of these children are poor. The overall poverty rate for children living in a grandparent's home is 27 percent; for children living in their parents' home, it is 19 percent. One-half of grandchildren living in a grandparent's home are younger than 6.

With respect to one-third of the children who live in a grandparent's home, the grandparent(s) lacks a high school diploma. In contrast, only one-eighth of children residing in their parents' homes can say the same thing about their parent(s).

CHAPTER EIGHTEEN

FOSTER CHILDREN/ADOPTION

"Foster care" is the term used for a system in which a minor who has been made a ward is placed in the private home of a state-certified caregiver referred to as a "foster parent."

The United States has a system of foster care by which adults care for minor children who are not able to live with their biological parents. In fiscal year 2000, 150,703 foster children were adopted in the United States, many by their foster parents or relatives of their biological parents. The enactment of the Adoption and Safe Families Act in 1997 has approximately doubled the number of children adopted from foster care in the United States. If a child in the U.S. governmental foster care system is not adopted by the age of 18 years old, the child is "aged out" of the system on his/her 18th birthday.

The state via the family court and child protection agency stand in loco parentis to the minor, making all legal decisions while the foster parent is responsible for the day-to-day care of said minor. The foster parent is remunerated by the state for his/her services.

Foster care is intended to be a short-term situation until a permanent placement can be made:

• Reunification with the biological parent(s)

o   When it is deemed in the child's best interest. This is generally the first choice.

•   Adoption

o   Preferably by a biological family member such as an aunt or grandparent.

o   If no biological family member is willing or able to adopt, the next preference is for the child to be adopted by the foster parents or by someone else involved in the child's life (such as a teacher or coach). This is to maintain continuity in the child's life.

o   If neither above option is available, the child may be adopted by someone that is a stranger to the child.

•   Permanent transfer of guardianship

•   If none of these options are viable, the plan for the minor may enter OPPLA (Other Planned Permanent Living Arrangement). This option allows the child to stay in custody of the state and the child can stay placed in a foster home, with a relative or an Independent Living Center or long-term care facility (for children with development disabilities, physical disabilities, or mental disabilities).

There were 547,415 children in publicly supported foster care in the United States in September 2000. In 2009, there were 423,773 children in foster care, a drop of about 20% in a decade.

In 2009, there were about 123,000 children ready for adoptive families in the nation's foster care systems. African-American children represented 41% of children in foster care. Caucasion children represented 40%. Hispanic children represented 15% in the year 2000.

Children may enter foster care via voluntary or involuntary means. Voluntary placement may occur when a biological parent or lawful guardian is unable or unwilling to care for a child. Involuntary placement occurs when a child is removed from his/her biological parent or lawful guardian due to the risk or actual occurrence of physical or psychological harm. In the United States, most children enter foster care due to neglect.

With all the benefits of the foster care system, there are some drawbacks as well. Individuals who were in foster care experience higher rates of physical and psychiatric morbidity than the general population. The incidence of depression, 20% as compared to 10% (those note in foster care) and were found to have a higher rate of post-traumatic stress disorder (PTSD) than combat veterans with 25% of those studied having PTSD. Children in foster care have a higher probability of having Attention Deficit Hyperactivity Disorder and deficits in executive functioning, anxiety as well other developmental problems. These children experience higher degrees of incarceration, poverty, homelessness, and suicide. Recent studies in the U.S. suggest that foster care placements are more detrimental to children than remaining in a troubled home.

CHAPTER NINETEEN WHAT

ABOUT OUR CHILDREN?

There were 92,854 young peope held in juvenile facilities as of the 2006 Census of Juveniles in Residential Placement (CJRP), conducted by the Office of Juvenile Justice and Delinquency Prevention. A "juvenile delinquent" is a person who is typically under the age of 18 and commits an act that otherwise would've been charged as a crime if s/he were an adult. Juvenile delinquency refers to antisocial or illegal behavior by children or adolescents. Most legal systems prescribe specific procedures for dealing with juveniles, such as juvenile detention centers.

There are different theories on the causes of crime, most if not all of which can be applied to the causes of youth crime. Youth crime is a major issue and is an aspect of crime that receives great attention from the news media and politicians. The level and types of youth crime can be used by commentators as an indicator of the general state of morality and law and order in a country, and consequently youth crime can be the source of "moral panics." Theories on the causes of youth crime can be viewed as particularly important within criminology. First, this is because those aged between fifteen and twenty-five commit crimes disproportionately. Secondly, by definition any theories on the causes of crime will focus on youth crime because adult criminals will have likely started offending when they were young.

An estimated 2.3 million children in the United States have a parent in prison—children whose lives are filled with a unique kind of instability and uncertainty. These children are themselves victims of their parents' crimes, members of a neglected segment of our population who are potentially damaged by stigma and shame and who are at risk of being pulled into a vicious cycle of future criminality and deviant social behavior. Do you think that the family, or the lack thereof, has anything to do with our kids being incarcerated? Do you think that if there were a strong father or father figure in the lives of these children, that it would affect their outcome?

Yes. Family factors which may have an influence on offending include the following: the level of parental supervision, the way parents discipline a child, parental conflict or separation, criminal parents or siblings, parental abuse or neglect, and the quality of the parent-child relationship (Graham & Bowling 1995). Children brought up by lone parents are more likely to start offending than those who live with two natural parents. However, once the attachment a child feels towards the parent(s) and the level of parental supervision are taken into account, children in single-parent families are no more likely to offend than others (Graham & Bowling 1995). Conflict between a child's parents is also much more closely linked to offending than being raised by a lone parent (Walklate 2003). If a child has low parental supervision, s/he is much more likely to offend (Graham & Bowling 1995).

Many studies have found a strong correlation between a lack of supervision and offending, and it appears to be the most important family influence on offending (Farrington 2002) (Graham & Bowling 1995). When parents commonly do not know where their children are, what their activities are, or who their friends are, children are more likely to truant from school and have delinquent friends, each of which are linked to offending (Graham & Bowling 1995). A lack of supervision is connected to poor relationships between children and parents. Children who are often in conflict with their parents may be less willing to discuss their activities with them (Graham & Bowling 1995). Children with a weak attachment to their parents are more likely to offend (Graham & Bowling 1995).

Delinquency Prevention is the broad term for all efforts aimed at preventing youth from becoming involved in criminal or other antisocial, activity. Increasingly, municipalities are recognizing the importance of allocating resources for the prevention of delinquency. It is often difficult for states to provide the fiscal resources necessary for good prevention, organizations, communities, and municipal governments are working more in collaboration with each other to prevent juvenile delinquency.

With the development of delinquency in youth being influenced by numerous factors, prevention efforts are comprehensive in scope. Prevention services include activities such as substance abuse education and treatment, family counseling, youth mentoring, parenting education, educational support, and youth sheltering.

CHAPTER TWENTY

MAN UP
(A Hard Pill To Swallow)

There is a popular (or unpopular) saying among some of the fellas I know. We use this phrase when we need to step up mentally our game, or when we need to suck it up and handle our business and do the things that we are supposed to do. We also use this phrase as a way to motivate each other to action and that simple phrase is "Man Up!"

That is the message that I have for the millions of men out there that need to do more, and even if you don't have children of your own, this message is still applicable to you. Our sons and daughters, nephews and nieces, grandchildren and neighbors are in a desperate need of positive male role models. Gentlemen, we need to "Man Up!"

There are certain parts of the entertainment industry that has attempted to teach our daughters that they are nothing more than bitches, whores, round-a-way girls, hood rats, ghetto girls, sluts, tramps, sex toys, and the like. Men, we need to "Man Up!" That same influence is teaching our boys and young men that the meaning of success is to have a Bentley they can't afford, a pocket full of money they didn't earn, gold teeth with no dental plan, and a pistol and a bag of weed in their backpack instead of books. "Ride or die" is a theme these young people have intergrated into their thought process. Men, we need to "Man Up!"

While working in the elementary schools, I can't tell you the number of second and third graders who knew all the lyrics to the latest songs on the radio, but could barely read and write. Men, we need to "Man Up!" I've watched our babies in kindergarten and first grade be suspended from school because they were "out of control." When the administrators call home, they are told by momma, "I can't do anything with them." When parents are called for intervention and help, it's usually a mother or a grandmother who responds, with no father in sight. When asked where the fathers are, the answer is almost always the same: They are in jail, dead, or not in the child's life. Men, we need to "Man Up!"

Our kids need to witness more of what to be. They certainly see enough of what not to be. Our sons and daughters need to see more men going to work rather than to court or prison. They need to see more in college than on parole or probation. They need to see more men taking care of their families than taking care of their habits or the drug dealer.

I love music as well as the next person, but the world really doesn't need another rock star or rapper. What we really need are leaders, such as business owners, inventors, poets, scientists, lawyers, police officers, educators, judges, nurses, and doctors, mechanics, musicians, engineers, plumbers, electricians, and the many other honorable occupations that are so desperately needed. They must know that there's more to life than a set of rims, a new pair of sneakers, and an i-Pod. Men, we need to "Man Up."

It has been said that if you want to kill any living organism you don't cut off the tail or trim its limbs, you cut off the head or pull it up from the root. The family is a living organism, and, if that family is missing its key ingredient, it's head or root, if you will, it will most definitely struggle and in many cases die. It won't always perish, but it will most certainly struggle to reach its fullest potential. Sure, there are success stories to be found here and there, but for the masses there is only despair and disappointment for those boys and girls who fall victim to poverty, HIV, gang violence, teenage pregnancy, and an outrageous high school dropout rate. We need to "Man Up."

Our "baby mommas" will struggle. Our wives and ex-wives will struggle. Our mothers and grandmothers will struggle. Also, our sons and daughters, grandchildren, and great- grand-children will also struggle. Men we need to "Man Up."

I know a great number of women have come to the conclusion that they don't need a man; who can blame them? I was talking to a friend who happens to be a single mom, and like many mothers she is doing a wonderful job with her children. When asked why she was alone, she told me that she could do bad all by herself! How did she come to that conclusion? What happened along her life's journey that forced her into that "I'm good all by myself box?" We need to "Man Up."

I have a neighbor and friend whom I admire very much. She is a woman of great poise and wisdom and someone I truly love and respect. She has two adult children in their mid-40s that she cares for very deeply. Like many women these days, she is a divorcee and was pretty much left to raise her children on her own with no help from their father. Her ex-husband is a person with notable social standing in the professional world and is highly respected in the community and beyond. But that respect and adoration are not reciprocated within his own family; within the walls of his own home, he has failed miserably and is all but hated by his own children. She, like countless other women, have been carrying around the hurt and pain left by a broken mar-riage.

To some degree I believe that my friend has gotten over her divorce, but her adult children are still suffering and strug-gling with a father they never really had. Her son is probably the most hurt and bitter man I have ever met! He has yet to for-give his father for what he did or did not do for him, his mother, and his sister. It has now been well over 30 years since their Adam has been gone, and the pain and disappointment still re-main. I have known their wonderful mother for over a decade now, and during that time I cannot recall one instance where the conversation of her ex-husband and her broken children have not come up. This concern and burden seem to be a part of her

DNA, but somehow, like many women, she has managed to pick up the pieces of her life and move on, but they are just that, pieces.

This chapter is not for women; it's for the men, the men who are supposed to be the leaders in our homes and communities. We are supposed to be the ones on the front lines for our families, not our women. Our responsibility is to honor them, to protect them, to provide for them, to make a way and intercede and be a covering for them. On the contrary, we are not supposed to abuse them, misuse them, abandon them, disregard, and denigrate them.

Pastor Jennings, my pastor, once said that hurt people hurt others. I believe that to be true. I also believed that it's virtually impossible to give what you do not have. How can a person love completely if s/he hasn't been taught how to love? There has to be a source. They have to learn it from somewhere. Desire is a wonderful thing, but it's not enough. You need a blueprint, a guide. If not, the house you are attempting to build will most definitely have a deformed foundation and many empty rooms. If I've learned anything in life, it's not the structure that's most important; it's the foundation. Men, we are supposed to be that foundation. If I were talking to friends, my message would be short and bitter sweet. That message would be: "It's time to Man Up!"

CHAPTER TWENTY-ONE

MY ROSE GARDEN

(A flower, no matter how beautiful the petals and how pleasing the aroma, is of no use to anyone when it's gone.)

As Father's Day was approaching, my kids (including Osai) asked me what I wanted as a Father's Day gift. Well, instead of risking getting another pair of argyle socks or another trendy tie, I asked them to write a chapter for this book. I only requested that they share their experiences and their true feelings. They were asked to give their perspective, a perspective that I could not duplicate and only they could share with the readers since this was what they had observed as sons and daughters. No other instructions were given to them. What you are about to enjoy is what they have decided to share, unedited and unchanged by me in anyway. So put on your comfortable shoes and let's take a walk, a walk through my rose garden.

CHAPTER TWENTY-TWO

FOLLOW THE
YELLOW BRICK ROAD
By Quion Wheeler

When asked to write this portion in my father's book, I was afraid that I would run out of room to type because one thousand words just isn't enough to begin to describe him. All of my life, I've had what some might say the perfect role model a young man could ask for, and I couldn't agree any less. As a child it took me a while to understand the whole parenting thing, I hated getting disciplined. I hated getting slapped in the back of my head in public. I definitely hated getting embarrassed in front of my peers. My father made it clear that he wasn't my friend; he was a parent first. During my younger years, I got in minor trouble, but every kid does. It's part of growing up and living in a house full of females with the exception of me and my father; you would understand. As the only boy in the house, I pretty much took all the heat for anything that went on dealing with trouble, and I'd have to say it's made me in to the young man I am today. I would consider my father to be a very stern, funny, hard-working, busy, do-it-yourself kind of guy. He'd try and figure out anything before actually going to the store to make a purchase. He has shown me how to do just about everything ranging from cutting the grass to changing a tire. These are things I feel that are beneficial and necessary growing up into a young man.

I remember, when I was growing up, my father would

give me tasks. I would always try to figure it out myself first before forcing myself to ask him. I hated not being able to complete a task, but I guess that's a part of learning. There are many things my father instilled in me, but some things that have always stood out to me were: "Birds of a Feather Flock Together," "Always Respect Adults," "Respect Your Mother," "Family First," and many other things. I carried them all the way from my childhood to now. I've always been blessed to have a father figure in my life because I have had a chalk outline on what a man is supposed to be like by watching him all these years. Fathers are important in a man's life because there are just some things a woman can't teach. Being a man is one of them. There's a big difference between being a dad and being a father. I say this because a dad is just a primary title given to someone who had a child; a father is a never-ending role that takes time, effort, and love in which my father shows daily. I'm sure there are times when my father wants to just throw in the towel, but he never does. He's always there, and he's never been absent in my life. I couldn't imagine what it would be like not to have a father around to see me do well in school, support me in my endeavors, help me fix my mistakes, and teach me how to treat women. There are a lot of young men out in the world who don't have anyone to teach them these things. As a kid I've always been in fear of making my father unhappy or failing. I've always wanted to show him that I can get the job done without his help. This explains why I try so hard to get it myself because my father always said, "You have to work before you play." For the longest time it took me awhile to understand what that statement truly meant. My priorities have always been tangled up. I was so used to putting things that weren't important in front of things that were. I guess you could say being a man is about making necessary sacrifices to take care of family and business.

Growing into my teenage years approaching college, I felt a slight distance between my father and me. I began to have curiosity amongst other things. Out of all things in life, communication is one of the key essentials in succeeding in any relationship, and, during that particular time, we weren't communicating much at all. For some odd reason, I was nervous to talk about things with him. I never gave it a shot until I realized I really needed his input on how to fix things and where I was headed in my life. Eventually, I swallowed my pride and just began to speak my true feelings and issues with my father. Despite it all, he never once judged me. He accepted me fully. It was almost as if he already knew the things I was going to say. In situations like this, I always admired my father because he was so forgiving. He always knew the right things to say to make me feel whole again. I believe this is a feeling I will always have about my father no matter how old I get. A father is important throughout your whole life. There is always something to be learned through all the wisdom he's encountered through life, and God willing, he's around to do the same for my future kids. I'm blessed because I know I have a father that's God-fearing , well-connected in the community, loving, a good husband, a great role-model, a leader, and a productive business man. These are all wonderful things, and I wouldn't trade my father for all the money in the world because it still wouldn't add up to the wonderful man he has become.

Through all the disagreements, punishments, pep talks, bike rides, vacations, and my whole life, my dad has always been here for me. It wouldn't be right if I weren't here for him during this time while he's writing this book. I love you. My friends love and admire you. I was honored even to be able to share a few of my personal thoughts about you in your book. With all being said, "Keep the faith and Keep on Keeping on." You are a blessing, and God will always continue blessing you.

Love, your son,

Quion Latrelle Wheeler

CHAPTER TWENTY-THREE

MY FATHER'S A KEEPER
By Quiana Wheeler

Last night I was involved in a lemon squeeze, something that my University of Michigan buddies made up my freshman year. A lemon squeeze is when you get groups of people together and basically share your story, whether it's good or bad. This gives everyone the opportunity to get to know the other person on a deeper level. My dad calls it "cutting to the chase."

As we shared our stories, I noticed that everyone's was different and unique in her own way. There was one particular girl whose story struck me! She told me that she was jealous of me, and in my mind I couldn't understand why. As I began to listen to her story, it all began to make sense why she felt the way she did. "Quiana," she said, "you have both of your parents in the same household." She then shared with me how she met her father. One day, she and her mother walked to their neighborhood market. As they were about to leave, a man pulled up in a car that she didn't know, and her mother told her that he was going to give them a ride home.

She told me that this awkward ride home became worse, as she noticed that the stranger kept looking at her in his rearview mirror. On one occasion she could swear she thought that he looked like he was going to cry. When she and her mother were dropped off at home, this stranger drove off, not to be seen again. Her mother then told her that that stranger was her father. That's how she met or didn't meet her dad, an un-planned ride home from the store. Telling me this story was a difficult thing for my friend to do, but somehow she seemed to find a sense of relief finally to share it with someone. That's what lemon squeezes are all about. Getting it off your chest.

As I look at my generation and many of the lives around me, it's very rare that there are two parents in a household. It's always the mother but never the father. I was often placed into an abnormal category by many of my peers because of what God blessed me with. I couldn't relate, but did I really want to? She mentioned to me that she wished she had someone to tell her she was beautiful or buy her a pretty dress or comfort her when she was down. Like the song says, "She was looking for love in all the wrong places." "I just needed somebody there to fill that empty space," she said. She wanted validation from men who didn't have her best interest at heart!

Listening to her story brought me to tears. The things she had gone through and the things she allowed others to do to her were things no young lady should have to experience. When I think of myself, I would have NEVER allowed someone to do to me what she has allowed others to do to her. My dad raised me to be an independent goal-driven woman. He always encouraged and supported me in whatever it was that I wanted to do. He has taught me never to depend on a man for happiness but to put all my faith in God and in His good works. I'm getting teary-eyed as I think about her story. If she only had a piece of what I had, her life would be so different. As I shared words of encourage-ment to her, she stopped me in my tracks and said she had been praying for a friend like me.

Another friend of mine and I were out to dinner one night talking about the significance of having a male role model. We concluded that it was important to have a father figure in your life. So we came up with this quote, a quote that I shared with this young lady: "My Father is a king, always treated me like a princess so no other man could treat me as anything less, in hopes that one day a king who aligns himself with the Almighty King will find me, and together we'll rest on our throne with me as his Queen." This beautiful young girl broke down and cried uncontrollably. How significant are those words?

Now that I'm older, I've finally accepted that being a good parent isn't always an easy task. I can say that my brother and I were a contributing factor of why my dad kept his bald head. He always made it clear that he was our parent—first—friend later. My father is a man that wears many hats. He's a wonderful father, dedicated husband, business man, karate instructor, friend, mentor, motivational speaker, minister, and, most importantly, a child of God. My hat goes off to him. I often ask my dad how he does it. He is involved heavily in the community and in so many people's lives, and he's always helping and encouraging others. Everyone seems to know him. I couldn't deny him as my father even if I wanted to. All they have to say is, "You're a Wheeler."

One of the many things that I appreciate about being my father's daughter, aside from the fact that he is already incredible, is that he values his family. He always taught me and my brother that family comes first and to work first and play later. He instilled that in us when we were younger so that, when we grew up, we would have a proper understanding of how things should be. My father's relationship with my beautiful mother is something that I admire and respect.

They share a love that is very rare these days. They've been married for 25 years and known each other for a total of 30. I can tell they still love each other because they're always kissing, which often times disturbs me. Yuck! But anyway, their marriage is a great example of what every marriage should be like and one I hope to have someday!

As a young girl, and still to this day, my dad has done his best in exposing us to different things, like traveling, skiing, boating on the lake, roller skating, and going to different places that shined with excitement, culture, and good memories, and for that I am so grateful. As a young girl, we stayed active. We were always on our bikes, roller blades, swimming pools, and he even took me to Girl Scouts. How many fathers can comfortably admit or say that they did that? Well, he did it for me! The types of experiences that I shared with my dad have really broadened and shaped me into the young woman I am today. I consider myself a social butterfly.

My most favorite thing to do with my dad and family are to be out on the water on our boat. It's so relaxing and fun to do. It's important to spend time with the family as my dad always says. The fact that my dad can hang all of his hats up on the rack and kick back with me and the family is what means the most to me. I wouldn't trade my dad for anything in this world.

I will always and forever be my father's daughter,

Quiana Lynn Wheeler

CHAPTER TWENTY-FOUR

LIFE SAVER, ANYONE?

How do you thank someone for saving your life? What is the motivation for the person who jumps in front of that bullet that is not intended for him? What do you say to the person who sacrifices on your behalf and expects nothing in return? As the recipient of such compassion, the first question that enters my mind is "why me"? But let's not get ahead of ourselves.

My story begins in Brooklyn, New York in 1988. My mother was born and raised in the projects. She is the type of woman that you can put in any situation and she will find a way to survive. Unfortunately, she got involved with the wrong type of individuals, dropped out of school, and was introduced to drugs. My father, on the other hand, was born in Flint, Michigan. Similar to the same temptations, my papa was a rolling stone. There are several other children that he had outside of my two other siblings that he had with my mother, but, unfortunately, I don't have relationships with them. Nevertheless, he was a hard-working man who joggled three jobs to support his family. In 1991 he died of cancer, or so I thought. His true cause of death was discovered accidentally over a phone conversation with my older brother last summer. For 21 years of my life, I believed my father was a victim of cancer, but in reality he was a victim of HIV. After my father's death, my mother decided to leave drugs and New York behind and move to Flint, MI. This would prove to be one of the best decisions she ever made.

It is hard to comprehend the struggles that a male faces when he grows up without a father. The father is a critical piece to the puzzle that solidifies the development of a young man. Like the "corner piece," everything starts with him. Starting at a young age, boys learn about their bodies from their father. They tackle the complexities of puberty with the wisdom and experience gained from their dads. Like the "center piece," the father is also critical in the final stages of male development. He shows his son a picture of what to expect when he becomes a man. This picture is more of a road map that navigates the boy through life.

Losing my father has birthed a plethora of mixed emotions and confusion inside of me. Like a pregnancy, I am forced to carry this weight with me wherever I go. I am reminded of my situation every time I see a father and son together. Bitterness engulfs me when I think about all the things that I will miss. I think of all the love and wisdom I would no longer have the privilege to receive. I thought that because my father was gone, I would be forced to navigate the journey of manhood alone. Thankfully, I was wrong.

God has strategically placed individuals in my life to fill those voids that my father left. Men, such as Jeff Wheeler, Michael Wilson, Henry Bazemore, and Lamar Carson, have stepped up to the plate and helped me be the man I am today. As I think about the impact that those men have had on my life, it often brings me to tears.

A great majority of my development happened through my martial arts instructors, Michael Wilson and Jeff Wheeler. The greatest gifts that these men have given me are the ones that are not tangible. Through these men I have learned about the importance of character and integrity. They have challenged me to keep my commitments and follow through my promises. At the age of 14, Mr. Wilson gave me a key to the karate school to teach me how to be responsible. Little did he know that the key meant much more to me. The key was a symbol of proof that I belonged to something bigger than myself. It showed that he believed in my capabilities and my potential to be a leader. Before that day I never felt like I belonged to anything.

When Mr. Wilson moved to Arizona, Mr. Wheeler stepped in and continued my development. The student-teacher relationship quickly turned into a father-son relationship as time progressed. Even though he had his own family to love and provide for, he never treated me any differently from his own children. When we are together, he introduces me as his son, not mentee or family friend. Growing up my mother would use Mr. Wheeler's name as a source of discipline. When she got really upset, she would threaten to tell him if I didn't get my act together. In fear of letting him down, I would beg my mother not to tell him. He taught me about critical principles such as accountability. Since I was 16, I have worked for him at Double Dragon Tang Soo Do. While this decision was great for me, it may not have been the best business decision for Mr. Wheeler. Despite all the times when I could have been fired, he used those mistakes as opportunities to teach me about responsibility and leadership.

Out of all the life principles that Mr. Wheeler has taught me, the most important one is principle of mentorship. I've experienced firsthand the impact of a good mentor. I have felt the accomplishment to hear a man say, "I'm proud of you son." I have heard the stories of past mistakes and how they can affect your future. I have received favor for no logical reason except love. I often try to think of my life without the impact of strong mentorship. To be perfectly honest, I have absolutely no idea where I would be. Mentorship has truly saved my life. This brings me back to the question I asked at the beginning of this chapter, "How do you thank someone for saving your life?" On Father's Day I tried to answer that question in a letter I wrote to Mr. Wheeler:

Dear Dad:

You always tell me that your kids never say, "thank you," so here it is. Attached is a list of previously "owed" thank yous that should bring me out of debt. Thank you for giving me Quion's old bike when I was 11 years-old. Thank you for paying for all the martial arts trips over the last 11 years. You can put it on my tab. Thank you for not firing me all those times I came late to the Karate school. Thanks for getting me out of hand cuffs when I got into that car accident. Thank you for letting me know that cars need oil to run efficiently. Thanks for helping me pay to get my car fixed when I didn't listen. Thanks for all the times you had to come out and tow my car with your truck. Thank you for letting me drive your Chrysler 300 when I couldn't afford a rental car. Thanks for feeding me when I first moved out of my mother's house. Thank you for introducing me to Henry Bazemore that led to a full-ride scholarship to the University of Michigan. Thanks for not saying "I told you so" when I learned lessons the hard way. Thank you for everything.

While saying thank you is great, it doesn't seem strong enough to reflect the appreciation of solid mentorship. There are no trophies big enough to express the gratitude I have for my father figures. The best way to show them I appreciate their sacrifices is to become a mentor myself. If I can be half the mentor as Mr. Wheeler, then I can completely change someone's circumstances. Until then a thank you will have to suffice. Thank you for being both my "corner and center piece." Thanks for saving my life.

Your son,

Osai

CHAPTER TWENTY-FIVE

GRATEFUL

My dad and I have a close relationship, but, truth be told, I don't always like the things he tells me. I do them because he is my father, but I don't always like it. For example, the other day my dad overheard me talking to a friend about this boy who hugged me four times while we were at camp. I didn't see anything wrong with it, but, when my dad heard this, he told both me and my friend that wasn't appropriate behavior. He said that we have to make sure we carry ourselves in a way that boys will respect us, and, being 12 years old, I better not let that happen again. It was harmless, but I guess he's right.

It's good to have a father in your life to spend time with you and correct you when you need it. I'm very grateful because there are a lot of boys and girls that don't have a father to turn to. A lot of them will get into trouble and go to jail or worse because they don't have a strong father to guide them but not me because my dad won't let me go down that road. I am very grateful for having a father and mother in my life.

Love,

Quiara

CHAPTER TWENTY-SIX

MY HERO

When asked to write a chapter in my husband's book, I have to admit I was a little nervous. You see I'm not much of a writer. I'm more of a face-to-face kind of person. But this is what he wanted for Father's Day. It beats standing in line at a Father's Day buffet. When I was thinking of a title for my chapter, "Hero" came to mind because my husband is truly my hero. I don't think fathers get enough recognition for the things they do.

My husband and I were having a conversation about parenting, and we were basically encouraging each other for the roles we have both played in our children's lives. He agreed that a man can't teach his daughters how to be women, and I had to agree that a mother in no way can teach her sons how to be men. Case in point—as was the normal morning routine, my husband and I were getting ready to go to work. As we were about to leave the house, we noticed that our daughter had already left the house, but our son was still home. Well, of course, my husband asked him the obvious: "Why are you still home?" Quion tried to explain to his father that his twin sister (Quiana) caught the school bus, but he overslept. I need to pause here and say that both of our 10th-grade children have been warned by their father that if they missed the bus, that literally picks them up at our front door, they would find themselves walking the two miles to the high school, regardless of the weather.

As what seems to be the norm with girls, one warning was all it took, and our daughter got the message, but that boy, that was another story. He had to learn the hard way. The daily routine for him was to get up late and rush out the door as the bus was about to pull off. As mothers do, I would fuss until I was blue in the face, but, the next day, it was like Ground Hog's Day all over again. "Get up, boy," I would say. "You're gonna miss your bus," I would say. "And I'm not taking you to school if you do," I would say. Funny thing, my husband was always calm and cool and would never say a word. So when that dreadful day occurred that he actually missed the bus, I went right back into fuss mode: "See I told you that you were gonna miss the bus. Now, get your stuff so I can take you to school...." Well, before I could complete my sentence, my husband intervened and simply said, "Boy, get your book bag and get to steppin'!"

Now, let me explain. It was the beginning of winter, and, if you know anything about Michigan winters, it was beginning to get cold outside. It had to be a blistering 30 degrees out there. This didn't phase my husband the least. With Quion standing with his mouth wide open in disbelief, his father calmly repeated his command, this time with a little more attitude, pausing at each word for effect, "I-said, 'get-your-book-bag-and-get-to steppin!'"

Wait a minute! Didn't he know how cold it was outside? How was he gonna just make my baby walk two miles in the cold. This wasn't the old days when we had to walk to and from school in the rain or snow regularly. How was he gonna just make my son walk? I know what I said about fussing every morning, yelling until I was blue in the face, but that's my baby. And it was cold out there ya'll. I had to stop myself because I had forgotten about being angry with my son. I was now getting angry with my husband. How could he do such a cold-hearted thing? Making my son man up, who does he think he is!?!

Well, needless to say, Quion suited up for the long haul and headed out the door. Funny thing, my husband didn't seem the least bit bothered by it at all, while I was stressed out all the way to work. He was making my son walk in the cold. As a matter fact, he drove right by him as he walked to school. Ooooooo I was pissed! I started to turn around and give him a ride to school anyway, but thought the better of it.

It seems that Quion made it to school ok. He didn't get kidnapped by aliens or get run over or freeze to death. He was ok. An interesting thing came out of that situation. He was never late for the bus again, and you know what? My mornings became less stressful. No more yelling, no more fussing. No more empty threats. No more blue faces. As for my husband, he went on being his calm, cool, and collected self, waiting for the next lesson to surface. I guess he was right, and I was wrong. There I said it! It does take a man to raise one. I must say that my son is very responsible just like his father, and he's learning to handle his business without as much help as he once needed. If he takes the lessons he has learned from his father, a great one he will be. Thanks honey for being my hero.

Love,

Your wife

CHAPTER TWENTY-SEVEN

SHOE ON THE OTHER FOOT
(If it weren't for grace)

During the almost quarter century that I served as a police officer, I have had the opportunity to see a lot of unique and unusual
things in my career, some good and some bad. I've seen people
at their best when tragedy shows its ugly head, and, as you would
imagine, I've also seen people at their worst, sometimes for no
reason at all.

Of all the higher education institutions that we have in
our country, there are none that have a higher graduation rate
than UHK, the University of Hard Knocks. One thing that I had
to learn very quickly, if I wanted to survive the job with my mental faculties in place, I couldn't wear my emotions on my sleeve.
For one, it would do me more harm than good, and, two, there
would be those who would be more than willing to take advantage of any perceived weakness that I displayed. To maintain the
objectivity for the people I served, I had to shift gears from sympathy to empathy. Sympathy took me on an emotional roller
coaster that left me all but mentally and physically drained at
the end of my day, whereas empathy allowed me to still have a
level of compassion for people without the emotional baggage
that often accompanied it.

That brings me to this point. When you see a homeless
person standing on the corner, what goes through your mind? I

know what used to go through my mind: Get a job! Right? I did. When you see a group of boys roaming the streets when they should be in school or how about when your kids are behaving in such a way that makes you want to take off your belt and...,I am sure you get the picture.

It has been said that if you really want to get to know a person, you need to walk a mile in his/her shoes. Before you mis-judge the man or woman holding the sign on the corner, before we condemn that boy or girl, we need to trade places if not but for a moment. Empathy is an important quality to have when dealing with others. I have always taught my children to be com-passionate and thoughtful toward others because you never know what that person has gone through. Something that we seem to forget, that could be us.

I remember some years back I was with my children dropping off some videos at the local video store. I remember that it was the middle of winter and quite cold outside. We pulled up to the drop box where I observed a person standing near the entrance of the store at first looking a little suspicious. Once I looked a little closer, I noticed the lack of clothing the man was wearing, and his condition spelled very clearly that he was obvi-ously down on his luck. When I got out of my warm car, this stranger's eyes connected with mine. The man obviously felt that I was an opportunity for benevolence. He cautiously approached me with his hands in the air as if to present himself as harmless as possible.

As he got closer, I looked back at my children and saw concern on their faces as this mysterious stranger approached me. When we were within arm's reach of each other I could see in his eyes that he meant no harm. It was at that time that the conversation began and a meeting that I will never forget. This man shared with me that he was homeless not because he was lazy or on drugs but because he lost his job and benefits. His home, wife, and children soon followed suit. He then asked me if I could spare a dollar so he could get a hot cup of coffee down the road. Now, I know that we've all heard that line before, but this time it was different. To my kids' surprise, I offered him a seat in my car and offered to take him to a local coffee shop.

As we were traveling the icy roads, his conversation quickly shifted from his troubles to how good God was to him. How good God was I thought. How could this man with nothing to his name be thankful? He shared that even though he didn't have a permanent place to lay his head, he was still grateful. "Grateful for what?" I asked. He was grateful for life, the ability to see, hear, and feel. This homeless man gave my children and me a lesson that I won't soon forget. The lesson? To be thankful no matter what!

When we reached our destination, I was waiting for this man to somehow capitalize on the moment and attempt to gain more than the cup of coffee that he originally asked for, but that moment never came. After taking the dollar, he graciously thanked me for the ride and said goodbye to my children as he headed toward the front door of the coffee shop. As he was about to enter, I called out to him and asked him where he was going to bed down for the night. He told me that he had exhausted his stay at the local shelter, but would be allowed to return in 30 days. 30 days? He told me that as long as he was a paying customer he could stay in the coffee shop and keep warm. Well, I don't know about you, but a dollar doesn't go a long way these days so I gave him all the cash I had in my wallet which would cover him for a couple of nights at one of the strip motels. He assured me that my gesture wasn't necessary, but when I insisted he graciously accepted. The man who taught me a valuable lesson on thankfulness shook my hand, and that was the last time I ever saw him.

I don't claim to have a thorough insight to the mysterious man at the video store. Traveling a few miles in the comfort of my car is not the same as spending a day, week, or year with him in his struggle. But it was enough time to change my heart and thought process and not be so quick to jump to conclusions about people.

This story may not mean much to anyone else but me, but, when I think about being too hard on others who may have experienced a bad turn in life or maybe have not made the right choices, I remember that cold winter night at the video store. Conversely, when we see our young people making bad choices and doing stupid things, we need to remember some of the mistakes that we have made as kids and young adults and give them a break. But please, while you're giving them a break, don't forget to give them a hand.

CHAPTER TWENTY-EIGHT

THREE MONKEYS
(Hear No Evil; Speak No Evil; Speak No Evil)

As I write this chapter, another homicide has occurred with two more teenagers arrested for murdering an elderly man and stealing his pickup truck. This only contributes to Flint, Michigan's horrible reputation as it currently holds the title of the most violent city in the United States according to a quote by a MSNBC.com article written by Douglas A. McIntyre, Michael B. Sauter, and Charles B Stockdale. It gives the following information: Flint, Michigan—Population: 109,245, Violent crime per 1,000: 22, 2010 murders: 53, Median income: $27,049 (46.1 percent below national average), Unemployment rate: 11.8 percent (2.8 percent above national average)

The article states:

> The number of violent crimes committed in Flint
> increased for all categories considered for this list
> between 2009 and 2010. Perhaps most notably, the
> number of murders in the city increased from 36
> to 53. This moves the city from having the seventh-
> highest rate of homicide to the second-highest. The
> number of aggravated assaults increased from 1,529
> to 1,579, a rate of 14.6 assaults per 1,000 residents
> placing the city in the number one rank for rate

of assaults.

Flint Police Chief, Alvern Lock, is quoted as saying that he believed the city's violence stemmed from drugs and gangs. Flint has a relatively small median income of about $27,000 per household. The city also has a poverty rate of 36.2 percent. Does any of this move you? I think for most, it does not. It's just more information, another bad story, information that we are over in-undated with. It only affects those that it affects, right? Why should we be concerned about those statistics? After all they're just numbers. Well, I beg to differ. They're not just numbers; they're people, people who are going through, people who are suffering and struggling—people who are dying.

The other day, I was speaking with my brother in-law, Shun, a very successful entrepreneur and professional. We had a very interesting conversation. We talked about days gone by and how things have changed; it's funny, the older we get, the more we talk about days gone by. Anyway, I remember when I was a kid and I would hear older people talk about the "good old days." They would go on and on about the good old days. It was almost as if they were living in the past. I swore when I got older I would never do that. Well, guess what? Never say never!

Shun and I talked about life's journey and how we ended up where we are. We even shared some of our regrets. Funny thing about regrets, I've learned that no matter what we've ac-quired or accomplished in our lives, no matter how far we've gone, when it's all said and done, we can always reflect and find something that we could've done differently. Coulda, shoulda, and woulda. I guess that's where we get the term "hind sight is 20/20." I know I'm not alone in this. I think about how many things I would have done differently in my own life, if I only knew then what I know now. But, we can't spend our time looking in the rearview mirror of life; can we? That's not productive, nor is it healthy. If you're always looking behind yourself, you'll most certainly fall flat on your face as you move forward only to make more mistakes. Isn't it great that we can still make a dif-ference no matter where we are in life? We have to take what we have, what we have learned, and make the best of it. Sure, I could've made some different choices, but, for the most part, I think I'm doing ok and I'm sure you are, too. I read somewhere "If life has given you lemons, grab some sugar and make lemonade."

That's why we need people in our lives. We need people who are willing to help steer us around and over some of the bumps and bad spots that we're bound to encounter on our journey. They are kind of like bumpers in the bowling alley that keep the balls out of the gutters. That's what this book is all about, being a bumper for someone. Still, I must warn you. Some of those balls may leave a bruise or two, but it's well worth it in the end. Oh yeah, remember that bruises heal.

Well, the conversation with my brother in-law eventually turned to some of the thoughts in the book you're reading right now. He encouraged me to continue writing because he felt that this book was destined to help people of all ages who were struggling in their lives. I guess the struggle could be with where we are in our lives, how we got there, and where we hope to end up. One reason I believe that Shun could identify with my passion for this book is due to the fact that, along with some other dedicated men in the Sacramento, California area, they have created a mentorship program of their own. Surely, it will be an outstanding success. The program is created to reach for the hearts and minds of young people in the city of Sacramento, and beyond.

Anyway, he asked some questions, and I believe that these questions relate to the the very heart of this book—Where is Adam?: "How do we move people from their *desensitized state*?" "How do we inspire them to see the seriousness of the enormous problems involving our youth?" "How to get their heads out of the sand if you will, *and do something*!" I thought that these were great questions, not easy ones. These questions inspired me to write this chapter entitled the "Three Monkeys."

This chapter is not meant to insult anyone, so please don't be offended. It's meant to shine a light on a monster that has been living and breathing among us for many years. To put it into perspective, I'm reminded of a statue of three monkeys sitting on a ledge. They weren't bad monkeys. In fact, they were very nice monkeys, naive, but nice. They were impervious to what was going on around them. Life was good, and they had not a care in the world. But how could these monkeys live such a carefree life untouched by the devastation that was going on right in front of them? Well, one of the monkeys figured out if he covered his ears with his hands that he could ignore all the bad things that were being said. The other monkeys saw how peaceful their friend was, so they decided that they needed to do something to protect themselves from the world around them as well. So they got together and came up with a great idea! One would cover his eyes so he would not have to see the evil around him, and the other agreed to cover his mouth so he wouldn't repeat the evil he had seen. Together they figured they had it licked.

One refused to hear. One refused to see. One refused to speak. So the three of them had a pretty good life, immune to what was going on around them. The lesson for me in this metaphor is that all of us, if we're not careful. are susceptible to falling into the same trap. Denial is deceptively destructive; I also learned that ignorance is not bliss.

The solution? I don't think we can just wave our hand and people will miraculously appear out of the woodwork ready and eager to be a part of the many concerns that face us today. I also do not believe that gimmicks or guilt should be utilized to commandeer assistance. The way I see it, you must first present the issue in such a way that it moves from a person's head to his/her heart, then from a person's heart to his/her hands. The head will analyze, evaluate, and give the concern credence and value. The heart will put passion and purpose to it, and the hands will eagerly and effectively work it out.

The other day I was at work and was approached by Jo Jo, a friend and co-worker, that I allowed to read a couple chapters of this book. She along with others have been a great inspiration to me. Jo Jo and I exchanged pleasantries as we usually do, and she told me that she wanted to share something special with me. Like a kid with a secret she said, "Guess what I did last weekend?" What she told me next brought tears to my eyes. Not having a clue, I asked her what the surprise was, and she told me that over the weekend she had a visitor from the local Girls and Boys Club who stopped by her home for an interview and inspection. She told me that after reading the chapters about Joe, she decided she needed to <u>do</u> something to help someone else. Not having a ton of money, she decided that she could give of herself. As she told me this, I did my best to hold back tears that were forming behind my imitation Foster Grant sunglasses. <u>Jo Jo got it!</u> She didn't need a memo. She didn't have to have a forum; she just did it. That's what this book is all about—reach out and help someone. Reach one; teach one. If we touch just one young person, we can literally change an entire generation. Wow!

Whether it's the devastating effects of global warming, the benefits of recycling plastics, or illegal whaling in the Antarctic, the million-dollar question is: How do we get people to care enough to get involved? We know that mere information is not enough because we are bombarded with information every day. How many times have we watched an infomercial about world hunger and the need to save a pet or pleas to donate to a disaster- stricken area only to turn the channel. Sometimes, we respond, and, sometimes, we don't. But when we do respond, what is it that caused us to do so? Was it because we felt that that particular plea or situation was worth getting involved with? Was it guilt? What was it?

Sometimes, I find that we think that the problems are so large and beyond our reach, that there's nothing that any one person can do to make a difference. We sometimes have to be reminded that the longest journey begins with just one step. All it takes is one person taking the initiative, one person like Dr. Martin Luther King, Jr. to stand up and say, "I have a dream."

It was John Wooten who said, "Don't let what you cannot do interfere with what you can do." Norman Vincent Peale said, "People become really quite remarkable when they start thinking that they can do things. When they believe in themselves, they have the first secret of success." Thanks Jo Jo, for teaching us to be monkeys no more.

CHAPTER TWENTY-NINE

QUESTIONS & ANSWERS

I thought it would be interesting to have a little question and answer session with various individuals from different walks of life. Some of whom I happen to know very well and others not quite as intimately. Still, there is one commonality that they all share. I respect each and every one of them. The questions were answered by judges, attorneys, social workers, ministers, married fathers, divorced fathers, single moms, and married moms. I tried to cover every lane of society.

I wanted to know and share with you what these special people thought about this topic that is near and dear to me. To do so I formulated a series of simple questions that would be sure to draw some thought-provoking answers.

Listed here is a result of the questions that I posed.

<u>I have had the pleasure of speaking with a young father of three. His name is Sandy.</u>

Q.   What is the single most important thing that you can do for your children?
A.   *I think the single most important thing I can do for my chil-*

dren is to support and encourage them, to plant seeds into their lives and convince them that they can be whatever they want to be.

Q.   What do you think is the worst thing you can do?

A.   *To abandon them. Even though my mother and father divorced when I was younger, they were always there for me. I will never abandon my children.*

<u>I spoke to Anthony who is a married father with a son.</u>

Q.   What is the most important thing that you can do for your child?

A.   *The best thing that I can do for my son is to prepare him for life so that he can take care of himself. To make sure that he is educated and equipped for the world and to teach him to be balanced. My father told me that you're not a man until you can take care of yourself. The worst thing that I could do is abandon him, to be absent from his life.*

<u>I asked Anthony to take off his father's hat and put on his attorney's hat.</u>

Q.   As an attorney, what do you think is the main contributing factor that would explain the number of defendants that come through the courts?

A.   *Without a doubt single-parent homes, there is simply not enough fathers to guide and instruct these kids. Most of the people that come through the system come from unstructured, undisciplined homes. Education is not a priority. Most of the young people that I deal with have very little parental support, and without that support they have a much more difficult time staying on the right path. In my opinion, it's not more jails or stiffer sentencing guide lines that's needed; its parenting! I would say at least 70% of my cases involve those from single-parent homes.*

I asked Nik, the father of three, the same questions. He was short and to the point.

A.   *Being there is not enough. You have to show your children that you love them, and that includes correcting them when they're wrong and guiding them. The worst thing I could ever do to my kids is neglect them. It's my responsibility to be an example to them so that they can have a model. I don't want my kids to be lost. I play with them and I pray with them.*

I talked with childhood friend, Donald, a divorced and remarried father (and grandfather) of two young adult daughters.

A.   *Learn from God how to raise your kids because we really don't know how. And we need His help. We must always be there for them. When and if a divorce occurs, make sure that the kids aren't caught in the middle. That's the worst thing you can do. It's devastating to the children when the parents, married or divorced, don't get along.*

Q.   As a father do you have any regrets?

A.   *I have a ton of them. When you get remarried, make sure that your wife (or husband) has the best interest for your children. You have to take the time to make good decisions because children will be directly affected.*

I spoke to Tiffani, an unmarried mother of five.

Q.   What are some of the challenges you face as a single mother?

A.   *Juggling schedules and events while trying to give each child the attention and nurture they need. Making ends meet is another challenge I have, while attempting to keep the kids involved with some of the things they want and need to do. Because I have to work and go to school and fulfill my motherly duties, I'm not always around to make sure they are doing the things they are supposed to do which opens the door for them to get into trouble. Recently, my oldest son got arrested, and I had to help him with that situation. As far as my boys are concerned, they need their fathers in their lives because I don't know how to teach them to be men. I can try and teach them to be good people, but I'm not equipped to teach them how to be men. My eldest daughter has self-esteem issues and feels that no one loves her. A father in her life would give her identity and affirmation she needs.*

Q.   How was your relationship with your father?

A.   *My relationship with my father was pretty good but only because I pursued him. If he were in my life more as I was growing up, I probably would not have gotten into the trouble I did. I certainly would not have been a teenage mother.*

I spoke with good friend and mentor, Mike, who is a divorced father of one teenage daughter.

Q.   What is the best thing you can give to your daughter?

A.   *Teaching her who Christ is would be the most important thing I can do, even more than who I am. Not letting my daughter know how valuable and precious she is has to be the worst thing I could do. As far as regrets, I have many. The biggest is not being prepared and knowing how to be her father. Coming from a single-parent household and not having a male role model to point the way has made it a little difficult for me, but I'm still trying.*

Q.   Is there anything you would have done differently?

A.   *I would have a stronger circle of men in my life as well as hers.*

Q.   With your daughter living in Michigan and you in Arizona, how do you maintain your relationship with her?

A.   *That's a tough one. I need to be in her physical presence. That's as important as the verbal communication. You can't replace not being there for your kids. They need to know that you are there; they need to see you in the stands at their events. If I could say one thing to fathers, that one thing would be "man up and be the father your children need you to be."*

<u>**Sandy is one of my Karate moms, a woman I truly respect. She has had many challenges while raising her 10-year-old son alone. She is a tough, compassionate, and resilient woman left to raise her man child alone.**</u>

Q.   What do you think is the most important thing that you can teach your son?

A.   *The most important thing is to teach him how to be a contributor to society, to be a good person.*

Q.   What are some of the challenges that you have faced as you raise your son alone?

A.   *Having one income has been difficult. I've had to sacrifice so that my son can have the things he needs. That often means that I have to go without.*

Q.   What are some of the things that you are doing to insure that he has male role models in his life?

A.   *Taking him to karate and soccer is important. He needs to be around you and his male soccer coach to have that positive male influence. In school, I've even requested that he be transferred to a class with a male teacher. His dad has never really been there for him. He still remembers when his dad told him that he was going to call him on his 6th birthday and he never did. That's been over 4 years ago. My son is angry at his dad for not being there. I have him in counseling.*

Q.   What would be your idea of a good father figure for your son?

A.   *My idea of a good father is a man that is stable, supportive, and encouraging. He must know how to love his children. The children must know that they are loved.*

Q.   What are some of the challenges that your son faces without his father in his life?

A.   *When teachers and kids ask him where his father is, that's probably the most difficult thing for him. He sees others with their fathers. I know that it bothers him. He's a special kid despite his challenges.*

I had the pleasure of interviewing a Department of Human Services Regional supervisor.

Q.   What are some of the defining factors that explain your incredible case loads?

A.   *I would have to say the incredible numbers of single moms that we serve, the numbers are very high, around 70% and growing every day. People are hurting. You already have families that have been on some forms of assistance for generations—grandmothers and mothers and now their children. Still, the economy has forced many others to seek out assistance as well.*

Another problem I see are the numbers of young mothers that are in the system. They simply don't have the parenting skills. They leave their young children home alone. The abandonment and neglect cases we see are overwhelming, and, of course in most of these cases there are no fathers to be found. To add insult to injury, the cycle just repeats itself when their children have children. I don't know what we are going to do in the coming years. There is a law that will go in effect December of 2011 that restricts recipients to 48 months of aid life long; then, they will be cut off. There will no longer be life time and generational assistance available. There is going to be a rude awakening coming very soon. There's simply not enough funding available. Substance abuse is another huge problem.

Q.   What do you see as the answer?

A.   *We need more resources and support from the State! There are other agencies that are out there, but most people don't qualify. There needs to be a change. Also, there is no structure in the homes that we deal with. In many cases the children are running the house. They tell their mothers and grandmothers what they're going to do or not do. It's crazy! Another growing problem that we have seen is the number of grandparents raising their children's children. They are often not equipped to do this, but more and more are stepping up to the plate. The number of kids in foster care and other agencies is very high as well. They often suffer more problems in the care of these individuals, like physical and sexual abuse as well as neglect. The people that are supposed to help them, sometimes, are the ones hurting them. I must say, however, that most do not engage in these actions, but it does happen. They need their parent. That's the bottom line. Our job is very difficult. It's physically and emotionally draining.*

Q. In your opinion how important is the father in all of this?

A.   *You learn your life lessons from your father. He is the key. We all know that moms are important. That goes without saying. However, fathers are critical, too. They are the structure, the fortification, and the affirmation; they're what holds it all together. Mothers have a tendency to be too easy on their kids. That's where the fathers come in to bring about a balance. You gotta' have fathers. They need to step up!*

CHAPTER THIRTY HERE

COMES THE JUDGE

As I was bringing this book to a close, I wanted to end it with thought and insight from one of the most powerful and influential entities in American society: The Judge! Who would have more perspective and opinion than the Judge? Who would have observed more family dysfunction than the Judge? Who has seen more tragedy, more devastation, and social disregard than the Judge? Who would have more access into the lives of the hundreds and even thousands of broken people than the Judge? Finally, who has more authority to change the course and direction of those individuals, including taking away their freedom and even their very lives? You guessed it. The Judge.

As a police officer, my sole responsibility was to bring those to justice that were in violation of the laws of our city, state, and country. One of my other responsibilities was to present a presence with the hopes of deterring crime in the community. Any police officer worth the weight of his badge knew and understood the value of prevention. This was accomplished in many ways. Being connected to the community, creating contacts, and having an ear for those that would share vital information would allow me to stop the crime before it actually began. As important as my role was, it pales in comparison to that of the Judge. Because after the arrest and investigation has been completed, after the defense and prosecution have presented their cases, and after the jury has fulfilled its civic duty, it all ends up in the lap of the Judge.

I had the dubious honor of speaking with several of society's greatest defenders of the right—Community Activist and Circuit Court Judge Archie Hayman and District Court Judges Nathaniel Perry and William Crawford. These tremendous individuals were excited and eager to share their experiences and thoughts, as relates to the difficult but necessary positions they unselfishly occupy.

My first interview was with Circuit Court Judge Archie Hayman, a man that stood much taller than his 5'8" frame would suggest, a person I had not had a conversation with for at least two decades. When I was considering whom to interview, he was one of the first people who came to mind. What I remembered about him was that he was tough on those he sentenced but fair, convincing in his deliberation, but compassionate. As with the others, he is a person that I highly respect and count it an honor to include his thoughts in this book:

> Officer Wheeler this book is well overdue. This is something that every mother, every father, and every defendant that comes before my bench should have to read. One of the biggest problems I see is in the area of judgment. People are simply making poor choices and using bad judgment they don't take the time to analyze their situation befor making their decisions. For example, my deceased brother and I grew up in the same house, had the same influence, both positive and negative. I heard the same things he did, but I decided to make different decisions. For example, I knew that work was necessary. I saw my dad work very hard to take care of his family; I actually worked my way through school to become a lawyer. On the other hand, my brother did everything he could do to get out of work. I also held a different view of women than my brother.

His view of women was that they were supposed
to take care of him and doing drugs and all kinds of
things. He had no goals and, eventually, lost his job.
By the time he was forty-five, he had a heart attack
and died. I believe that his untimely death was a result of the choices he made. I'm certainly not saying
that I was better than my brother; I'm not saying
that at all, but I do believe that I made better choices.

A lot of young men are being raised under
the thought process of what can't happen for them
or what is unobtainable. Basically, they're being
taught failure. Here's what I learned. If a parent
goes to college, there is a strong chance that his/her
children will go to college. Likewise if a parent
goes to prison, the odds increase that one of their
children will also go to prison. It works both ways.
We know that isn't every case, but in my experience it happens more times than not. It really scares
me the numbers of men going to prison because I
know that it won't be long before I see their sons following in their footsteps. I've been in this business a
while and I've seen this happen more times than I
care to mention. I'm sick of it. I think this book may
help!

I believe that all children want to be with
their biological parents, no matter how dysfunctional the family may be; kids just want to be with their
parents. When I've done divorce cases, there were
those who would say that it doesn't matter if the kids
are with their parents as long as they're safe. I agree
that all kids should be safe, but from my perspective
it does matter whom they live with. If they're not
with their parents, you are going to see a lot of anger
and resentment. Then, you see them act out when
they get older and usually end up in my world.

The mother is very important, but that fa-
ther is critical in the life of his children because there

has to be someone who stands in the way of disaster, even someone who offers a threat. When I was a kid, my mom was the one who did most of the disciplining. But when my dad got home, we would get it again. As kids grow (especially boys), our mothers don't offer much of a threat physically anymore. The physical presence she once had is gone, so there has to be someone whom they see as the authoritarian, both physically and mentally. That father is that presence. It helped keep me in line. That's just a thought. Mothers have a tendency to be easier on their boys than their daughters, often enabling them. Also, that is a problem I see.

Most crimes are adult-generated either by action or through lack of parenting. When I get a 15 year old out committing crimes at two in the morning, you have to ask yourself: Why is this child out at that time of morning? Where are the parents? This is happening far too frequently. That wouldn't happen in my home because my dad expected me to be home when the street lights were on. If I were not, there were consequences. These kids don't have any consequences. When they do, it's too late. We also had the village concept in full effect when I was growing up. Nobody called the police on his/her kids when I was growing up. If my neighbors saw me doing something I wasn't supposed to do, they would get me, so I would get it three times, by my neighbor, my mom, and my dad. And I turned out ok. On occasion I was even sent to get my own switch when I was in trouble. That kind of stuff doesn't happen anymore. I know how some people feel about what we call "corporate punishment." I don't advocate abusing children, but we have a responsibility to discipline properly our children, and it must be done in love. The change that we so desperately need with our boys and girls, even our young men and women, rests within the family, not the courts.

I also spoke with District Court Judge William Crawford who also happens to be a neighbor. I have watched him along with his wife raise three wonderful children. On countless occasions I have seen him and his family walking or riding bikes in the neighborhood. I think that a father who spends time with his family is a wonderful sight to see. Judge Crawford was delighted to share his thoughts regarding his experience.

Q. Judge, in your opinion what is needed most to help reduce the number of people that come before your court?

A. *Jobs! When I was growing up, my father was the Executive Director of Big Brothers Big Sisters. At one time he had 20 little brothers and sisters. He was big in helping others find jobs. Also, I learned from him that position and status are not power; helping others is power. When you empower others, then you have real power.*

I believe that the economy is one of the main reasons people are in the condition they are in today. It is a major contributor to crime in not only our community but many other communities as well. We live in a town where the source of income and jobs for many years has been the automotive industry which at one time employed tens of thousands of people. Now, even with the so-called turn around, the numbers are nowhere near what they used to be. Other areas have suffered the same fate. Like steel mills and logging, those types of industries have all but dried up. As they diminish, so do their communities and the people in them.

Q. What kind of influence did your father have on you?

A. *I had a stable upbringing with a lot of traditional values and experiences, like going south during holidays and family activities. My father was a great example; he was big in helping and hiring others and treated everyone with respect.*

Q. As a father what do you think is the best thing that you can do for your kids?

A. *The best thing I can do for them is teach them to have self-responsibility, to take the initiative in the things they're supposed to do. To take advantage of opportunities that come their way and make the best of them.*

Q. What is the worst thing you can do or not do for your kids?

A. *Not to be there and not teach them that their choices have consequences because they do. Being there is a must! My father was there for me, and I am there for my kids. I was at the track the other day in the hot sun running, and I saw a young man that looked to be high school age working out. I noticed that he was doing some advanced drills so I asked him what he was preparing for. He told me that he was training for the varsity football squad. The drills he was doing he learned from his father. When I asked him where his father was, he looked a little disappointed and said that his father was no longer around, but he was still doing the drills that his father taught. I thought wow! This kid had enough sense to do what his father taught him even though he was no longer around. I can only hope that there are other lessons that his father taught him before leaving. The lessons our fathers teach us are very important and are lifelong.*

Q. Do many fathers come to support their children in your courtroom?

A. *For the vast majority of the cases, they don't, but there are a few that step up. Sometimes, the dads are actually the ones pressing the charges against their children. There are occasions that I see fathers who are upstanding and trying to do the right things for their children.*

Q. What word of advice would you give to fathers to help them to become better parents?

A.　*Get busy with the time that you have left! You want to be able to look back and say that you've done right by your children and understand that it's never too late to try. I've had mothers and fathers who come into my court room wishing that they would have done things differently. Many mothers and on rare occasions fathers have begged me to let their kids out of jail. When I've made the decision not to, those same parents have come back to me and thanked me for making their children serve out their sentences, telling me it was the best thing for them. Sometimes, locking them up for a spell can give them time to rethink what they've done. It works for some, but, unfortunately, it doesn't work for all. So my word is keep trying.*

And last but certainly not least, I had the pleasure of speaking with District Judge Nathaniel Perry.

Q.　What was your life like growing up?

A.　*I grew up in the segregated South and was raised by my mother, who's 94 now. My father left us when I was about four years-old; my mother worked two jobs to make ends meet. To keep me under control, she would say things like, "You don't want to be like your father" and "If you go to jail, don't call me!" I know she only told me those things to keep me focused. Many of my family members didn't have any real goals. There was a lot of alcoholism, so my mother encouraged me to do better. She used to push me to do well in school, which I did. There were some in my family that would criticize her for trying to do better. Even though she only had an 8th grade education, she wanted more for me. You know…it did not really dawn on me that I was in a single-parent home, because my mother did so much for me, she was my mother and my father. My mother remarried when I was about 8 years old. My step-father was around for about 5 or 6 years. He wasn't an educated man, but he taught me some valuable lessons, like how to use my hands. Men are important in their children's lives; they give them balance;*

they teach things mother can't.

Q.   Where did your biggest influences come from?

A.   *As I was growing up, the men in the church, my basketball coach in college, and my teachers had huge influences in my life. They taught me about character and integrity and gave me good advice. But I would have to say that the biggest influence was my ex-wife's father. I never really knew what family structure was until I saw him with his children. He was great! I can say that he taught me a lot about fatherhood. Because of watching him, I can say that I have only missed 3 out of 50 of my son's football games. I really tried to be there for my kids as they were growing up. And, of course, I'm still there if they need me even though they are adults. I learned a lot from that man.*

Q.   Can you tell us your journey to the bench?

A.   *Well, when I was in middle and high school, I aligned myself with the kids that were doing the right things academically. It paid off because I got accepted in a program that afforded me the opportunity to go to Fisk University. I am the first person in my family to graduate college. After graduating I moved to the Flint area and began teaching. I did that for about 10 years. Then, I decided it was time for a change. Then, I went to law school. After graduating I worked for the Prosecutor's Office for a while then went into private practice. In 1990 I ran for District Court Judge, and here I am. Since being on the bench, I've had the pleasure of serving as Chief Judge for two terms, and I also served as Presiding Judge. This has been an eye-opening experience.*

Q.   Shifting gears, Judge, what would you say would be some of the defining factors that contribute to the cases that come before your bench?

A.   *Babies having babies! These young people really don't have any idea what they're doing. They are young and inexperienced.*

They haven't been taught core values because they haven't been taught. They can't teach their children, so this causes them to make terrible mistakes. Many of these young parents haven't been properly parented themselves. They simply lack proper guidance.

My son is married with his own children. One day he called me about a situation that he was having, and he asked me my advice. Even though he is an adult, he knows that he can come to me for advice. It's my job to give him the best advice I can. Someone very close to me told me that he wasn't the smartest fella but he wasn't the dumbest either and, if I ever needed advice, all I had to do was ask. He also told me that I could count on him to give me the best answer that he could. I guess that's really all anyone could ask for. It's good to have people like that in your life. Most of the people I deal with haven't had that luxury.

Another problem I see is that the young people these days don't see the importance of being informed. Instead of watching programs that can educate and enlighten them, they watch stuff that gives them a false reality of life. Their value system is obscured. There's a lot of things they simply don't understand, something as simple as work ethic, for example. My mother told me that if it's worth having it's worth working for.

Q.   How does the missing father fit in?

A.   *As I mentioned earlier, the father brings about a balance for the children. He brings another perspective that a mother can't bring. Children need their fathers.*

Q.   What percentage of people come before your court are products from single-parent homes?

A.   *Eighty percent at least. There are a few fathers out there, but they are few and far between.*

Q.   If there were more fathers, would things be different?

A.   *Absolutely! It wouldn't change everything, but it would cer-*

tainly make a difference.

Q.   If you could tell fathers and men in general one thing to help them along their way, what would it be?

A.   *When dealing with youth, learn to listen and listen to learn. Don't be afraid to interact with young people just because they don't look like you or act like you or because they have tattoos and piercings. You don't know what they've been exposed to. Don't be deterred by their background or the language they use; look past that superficial stuff and touch their lives because they need us.*

You know the people behind bars weren't born to be there. They ended up there because of the bad choices they made. They either weren't guided, or they were misguided. It's very easy to judge people where they are. It's another thing to judge the process to how they got there. In my opinion how they got there is as important as how they arrived. I consider both in my courtroom.

In closing, I would like to say that it was my mother who gave me the foundation that I needed to start my journey, but it was the men that I was fortunate enough to have in my life that helped me complete my journey. My youth pastor, college basketball coach, teachers, step-father, and father-in-law, and others were all instrumental in helping me along this trek to manhood. When I think back, even my father, who left my mother and me when I was only four years old, had a positive influence in my life. Like most boys and young men, I was angry, angry because he wasn't there for me. That same anger has been one of the reasons thousands of young men end up in prison. It's sad to say, but the most important thing I learned from my father was not to be like him. I guess I learned to turn a negative into a positive.

***

I would like to thank Judges Hayman, Crawford, and Perry for taking time out of their busy schedules to share their wisdom, experience, and insight with us. I must share with you, that while I was interviewing each of them, their cell and office phones were ringing off the hook, but they were gracious enough to give me their undivided attention. Each judge could have filled a volume of books with the knowledge and experience that they have.

The people of this city, state, and country are fortunate to have such men (and women) of character and compassion sitting in such an important position in our society. Unfortunately, because of budget cuts in our state, many of these seats will be eliminated in the near future. I can only hope that our economy will soon recover, so that we do not have to lose many of the patriarchs that hold our social fibers together. We desperately need our judges, educators, law enforcement officers, as well as those in the civil and social fields to continue to fight for us.

If you have been touched in any way by this book, I would ask that you share it with anyone that you think may benefit from it. Single mothers and fathers, those that are married or divorced as well as sons and daughters, nieces and nephews will be challenged by this book. Youth groups and mentoring programs and the like may find this as a valuable tool that will be of great influence in bringing about positive conversation and solutions to this epic problem.

In the words of a good friend, "My time is up; I thank you for yours."

Jeffrey Wheeler

Life is but a moment; a moment is an opportunity;
an opportunity is a chance, a chance to make a difference.

CHAPTER THIRTY-ONE

HOW TO HELP
(A RESOURCE GUIDE)

Helping others is one of the most responsible and honorable self-less acts a person can do. Not only are you assisting someone in need, you are also making a difference, rebuilding your community one person at a time. One of the most difficult parts of volunteering is finding an opportunity that fits your personality and schedule, not just to talk about the problem, but to create solutions as well. One way to do that, if you are a man reading this book, extend yourself to a young person as that neighbor did to me. This will help you as a man to be a better father or a father figure to the many young people who are in need. If you are a woman reading this book, give it to your sons, daughters, your husbands, your "baby daddies," your brothers, sisters, or to anyone you think may benefit or be encouraged by it.

In this section I have listed a few resources for those who may want to lend a helping hand. Please don't limit yourself to my list. There are many ways to help kids and young adults. Most don't cost a dime, just a little of your time. Because of the Child Protection Act, you may be required to take a background check when working with public agencies such as schools and centers. Please don't be offended by the request. This ensures that our children are protected. Never forget the power of MENTORING. Now, go out and save a life!

You can help in so many ways:

1. Family members with children
2. Neighbors and friends with children
3. Take a young person to a ball game, a walk or bike ride, swimming, canoeing, skiing, hiking, fishing etc.
4. If you have a small business, hire a child and teach them the ropes
5. Local Boys and Girls Club
6. Big Brother/Big Sisters (thanks Jo Jo)
7. Volunteer in your local school, parent hall monitor programs, lunch aide or playground supervisor
8. Substitute Teach
9. Local Churches i.e. youth ministry, VBS etc.
10. Contact your local school and library about reading to children
11. Become a youth counselor
12. Form a youth group
13. You can help organize after-school mentoring or tutoring programs for disadvantaged or special-needs children. Speak with your school's administration on how to properly and effectively organize a solid mentoring program
14. Troubled Teens Crisis Programs, Boot camps
15. Collect children's books that are in good condition and donate to daycare centers or children's hospitals etc.
16. Youth Club Volunteer
17. Become a Coach or Sports League Volunteer
18. Teach chess
19. Teach music
20. Food and clothing drive for shelters that service youth
21. Contact your local Juvenile Court and ask how to help
22. Don't miss the mark mentoring program. M.A.R.K LLC, a children and adult mentoring program. Mr. Williams can be reached at dontmissthemark.net 810-6106194
23. Contact Shun Dickerson who sponsors a mentoring service at www.Makingaces.org.

My Notes.

ABOUT THE AUTHOR

Jeffrey F. Wheeler is married to Yvonna (TC). They have three children, Quion and Quiana (twins) and Quiara. Jeff is a product of a broken and often times dysfunctional home where there was plenty of domestic violence and alcohol abuse.

He was born and raised in the City of Flint, Michigan, a General Motors town that once bustled with life, business, opportunity, and prosperity, a town of close to 200,000 people in its heyday. It is now a town of barely 120,000 people, and a depleted city government with a school district that is barely holding on. But even though that once great city is hurting, its spirit is still strong and attempting to rebound from the ashes of an industrial crash and an unforeseen economic storm that has affected the once great city and the country as well. Jeff is proud to say that he attended public school and later the Full Gospel Christian Seminary where he obtained his License and Ordination to preach as well as a B.A in Biblical Studies. The Church and College are operated by his father, Dr. James L. Wheeler, Sr.

Jeff is a retired veteran of the Flint Police Department, where he served for some 23 years. He has performed duties as a patrol man, dispatcher, and community officer. He is currently an Instructor for the Flint Police Academy where he is a certified

Pressure Point control tactics instructor and also a Juvenile Law instructor. Since January of 1994 until his retirement in April of 2010, he served as a School Resource Officer for the Flint Community Schools, where he was a member of the Crisis Response Team.

He is a mentor to many, a motivational speaker, where he has engaged audiences at elementary, middle, and high schools as well as detention centers and various corporate agencies. He is the son of Pastor James L. Wheeler, Sr. and Delores J Stroud (Wheeler) and currently serves under Pastor Marvin A. Jennings, Sr. as an Associate Minister at Grace Emmanuel Baptist Church in Flint, Michigan. He has also served as Sunday School Teacher and Youth Leader serving hundreds of young people. He was also a volunteer for Big Brothers Big Sisters and the Boys and Girls Club.

Jeff is the owner and head Instructor of Double Dragon Tang Soo Do Academy in Burton, Michigan, a traditional Korean Karate school where he emphasizes character, discipline, and education. He is a repeat Regional and World Champion competitor and prides himself in helping others achieve their goals not only in the world of martial arts but in life as well. He has experience in other martial arts, but fell in love with Tang Soo Do many years ago and decided to make that his primary art. He is currently the senior most black belt in his region, and is pursuing his Master's rank within the World Tang Soo Do Association which was founded by Grand Master Jae Chul Shin. He recently wrote his 20,000 word thesis on the topic "The power of the Will"

In 2008 Jeff was honored and selected as the Karate Chairperson and Head Coach for the Flint Olympian and CANUSA International Goodwill Game which is a sports alliance between Hamilton, Ontario, and Flint, Michigan which began in 1958. That same year, the Detroit Pistons and The Boys and Girls Club of Flint honored him for his influence in the life of a young man. That young man, and The Boys and Girls Club re- ceived a scholarship from the Pistons organization for an essay that was entitled, "My Hero," which focused on his relationship with Jeff and the influence Jeff Wheeler had on his life. In 2014 Jeff was also selected and honored by the Alpha Kappa Alpha Sorority, Incorporated, Zeta Beta Omega Chapter as one of 12 men for the "Men making a Difference" in the community award.

As far as he martial arts school goes, when asked what led Jeff to open his own school.

He adds, that after observing the many terrible choices that young people were making, he decided to be a part of the solution. That solution was Double Dragon, which he opened on April 2, 2004. This was done only after much encouragement from his Regional Director and friend, Master Matt Ochs, a man that he respects and looks up to. He adds that there are many others that encour- aged him as he took on the challenge of opening his first school. People like Master Vance Britt, Master Mike Wilson, Lawrence Maclin, Mark Williams, Deacon Wesley Thompson, Mark Miller, Ronald Fitzgearld, and many others. His father and younger brother, James, Jr., proved to be his biggest allies as they pro- vided much help with not only the first school, but the second lo- cation as well. Jeff believes that iron does, indeed, sharpen iron, and birds of a feather do flock together. So he has surrounded himself with positive men from all walks of life; some are men- tioned in this book.

Jeff has made the acquaintance of men of great accom- plishment and social standing, ranging from mayors and other elected officials, professional athletes, successful business owners, school administrators, and other professionals. When asked who really sticks out in his mind as a powerful influence in his life, Jeff shares that there are many, but one man in particular stands out, a man with very little means. He wasn't in the corporate world nor was he a man with great substance; he had no portfo- lios, no 401ks or mutual funds. Even though he had very little to speak of in terms of worldly possessions, he was a great example of what a real man and father should and could be despite his circumstances. He was a recovering alcoholic who lost his job at General Motors. As a result of losing his job, he lost most of what he had, but, what he lacked in possessions, he more than made up with grit, integrity, and kindness. He has sinced passed away after a long bout with cancer. That man taught Jeff Wheeler to make the best of life with what one has and that an individual can recover from past mistakes even though s/he may have to pay for them later. He also taught Jeff to be the best man and father he can ever be and not forget to help others along the way.

So, instead of just putting handcuffs on the wrists of kids,
Jeff is proud to say that he is putting black belts around their
waists. Instead of his students becoming inmates and convicts,
he is teaching them to become instructors and coaches. He says
that this is his way of being a part of the solution. Jeff hopes that
this book will enlighten, encourage, and inspire others to find
their own way to help. There is a scripture that says "the harvest
is plentiful, but the workers are few." All we need is for one
Adam to stand up in each family, and the world will be a better
place.